Mainly Fun
and Horses

Mainly Fun and Horses

Rod Simpson
(with Russ Gascoigne)

Foreword by
Derek Thompson

MARLBOROUGH

MARLBOROUGH BOOKS
18b Ash, Kembrey Park, Swindon SN2 6UN

c/o 9 Queen Street, Melbourne 3000, Victoria, Australia

c/o 4 Arran Quay, Dublin 7

First published 1993

Typesetting and Origination Footnote Graphics, Warminster.
Jacket photographs *Phillipa Gilchrist*

Jacket Design *Ron Stephens.*

ISBN 1–873919–14–X Marlborough

FOREWORD

Rod Simpson is to training what John McCririck is to television – a real character. Like "Big Mac" he's also a true professional and whether he's working for charity which he does tirelessly or playing Sunday morning football with his great pal John Francome it's his horses who always come first. His total of winners in a season actually totals more than the number of horses in his stable and very, very few trainers can lay claim to that.

Even when his "good thing" gets beaten he still comes up fighting and thats what makes him special – he's a real fighter. He's had more than his fair share of knockout blows during his career but he's always pulled himself up off the floor and come back.

He's chirpy, cheeky and always buzzing and the wealth of racing stories that you'll find in this book will keep you chuckling all the way to the winners enclosure.

Derek Thompson

CONTENTS

THE HORSE GUARDS

When I come to think about it, I'm sure that one of the earliest signs pointing to which way my life was going to lead me came in 1952 or 1953 when I was about seven or eight years old.

An uncle and aunt took me to London for the day and one of the things we did was go and see The Horse Guards. They left quite an impression on me. I absolutely loved it. It was easily the highlight of the day as far as I was concerned. The swords, the saddlery, the plumed helmets. I loved it. The horses, the uniforms, the sheer spectacle of it all. It was such a sight. That's it, I thought. No doubt about it. That's what I want to be. I want to be in The Horse Guards. From that day on I was smitten. I used to go back to London whenever I could just in the hope of being able to see them all again. I even went on school trips there, although usually I hated doing anything like that. If there was a trip into London I'd always put my name down, always hoping that I might get the chance to see The Horse Guards again. And when I did my feelings were always the same. Always.

As a racehorse trainer I've gained a reputation for the sort of clothes I wear. Bright. Colourful. That sort of thing. Not what you usually find people in the profession wearing. And certainly not at the races – which is where I usually dress up all the more. When I was first starting out as a trainer I did it partly to get noticed. Simple as that. There was also the fact that I actually liked to wear yellow suits, pink suits, black-and-red striped trousers, whatever. "There's that so-and-so, Rod Simpson," I'd hear people say. It did the trick. It got me noticed all right. Another reason for doing it was that I wanted to stir things up a bit, make a bit of a splash in that respect too. Why, if you're a racehorse trainer, do you have to wear this uniform of the brown or green trilby, the suit, the brogues? Why not have a bit more showbiz, a bit more razzmatazz . . . a bit more colour? I think racing needs it. Of course, someone pointed out to me – and not so long ago, in fact – that all of this probably stems from my having been so interested in The Horse Guards when I was a kid. And certainly it wasn't so much the horses that I was interested in then as the uniforms. That was what really caught my eye, my imagination. I didn't want to join The Horse Guards so that I could ride a horse; I wanted to join so that I could wear that uniform, that was all. I haven't actually turned up at the races wearing a red plumed helmet yet, but who knows? One of my owners sent me a white stetson a while ago, a real ten-gallon job, with a spray of feathers in it . . . Perhaps I'm getting there.

It was still my ambition to join The Horse Guards when I was about fourteen or so. Trouble was, I was so small. I hadn't grown much since I'd first seen them. There was no way I was going to make it, I knew. I tried telling myself that I would grow – but I knew. There was no way. No chance. Not that they would have had me anyway. Perhaps I could work my way up by becoming a cadet or something, I thought. But of course I was kidding myself. There was just no way. No way at all. I was too small and people like me just didn't get to join The Horse Guards.

At about the same time we were given a questionnaire at school, asking us what we wanted to do when we left. I wrote down that I wanted to join The Horse Guards anyway. The reaction I got from the teachers, of course, was all along the lines of "You know this is absolutely stupid, don't you?" And it was true; I did. But that was what I wanted to do. Joe Bloggs put down fireman, someone else

10

put down window cleaner or whatever. I put down that I wanted to join The Horse Guards. Never mind how stupid it might be.

And then one of the teachers, a P.E. teacher, Mary, asked me if I liked horses. I told her that I'd hardly ever seen one – apart, that was, from when I'd seen The Horse Guards. My grandfather had had a milkcart that was pulled by one and that was it. That was all the contact I'd ever had with them. I'd spent almost all of my childhood in Croydon and there just weren't many horses around. "The thing is," she said. "We think you might make a good jockey." I was good at sports at school, not much else. Cricket. Football. Cross-country running. You name it. Again though, the trouble was I was so small. I was never going to be that good simply because of my size. As a jockey, on the other hand, not only would my fitness be of advantage but my size would be my biggest asset of all.

Good idea or not, I didn't really give her suggestion much thought at the time. You don't really give anything that much thought at that age. Even so, she kept on asking me about it. She told me that her fiance's father had a couple of hunter chasers at home and that she and her fiance often rode them. She invited me to have a go myself, see how I got on. The thing about Mary was, she was so encouraging. She had a really nice way about her and would always try to bring out the best in you. Finally, then, I did give her suggestion some serious consideration. I had to. The first thing that struck me was that the thought of me being a jockey seemed almost as stupid as the thought of me joining The Horse Guards. But Mary wouldn't give in. Eventually, she convinced me that I should at least go riding with her to see whether or not I liked it. If I didn't like it, okay. No big deal.

So off I went to her future father-in-law's in Banstead. And it was there that my lifelong involvement with horses began.

In a way, all because of those Horse Guards.

11

A CROYDON KID

Perhaps it was just as well that I didn't get into The Horse Guards. I may well have discovered that it was only the uniform that I liked. Truth be told, if I had gone into The Services, The Navy might have been a better option for me – even if the uniform wouldn't have been anywhere near as eyecatching. The thing is, I love the sea. I always have. I've got a small 'summer' house near Looe in Cornwall and I go there whenever I can. I've got a small boat there and I can't get enough of just messing about in it. I go swimming, fishing and water-skiing. Well, I'm learning to ski; I don't get to spend anywhere near as much time as I'd like down there, so diving is probably a more accurate description of what I do. No sooner am I up on the skis than I'm straight back in the water again. Useless. But I thoroughly enjoy it. I just love being by the sea. In it.

Anyway, as well as nursing an ambition to join The Horse Guards I did once consider joining The Navy. My father, who had previously been a silversmith, served in The Navy for a short while during the war. He then joined The Merchant Navy and served out the rest of the war there. During his stint in the former he was a gunner . . . aboard one H.M.S. Rodney. That, of course, is where I got my name from. Perhaps it runs in the blood or something, but I thought I'd like to go to sea too. I could imagine myself as a sailor – and the uniform had nothing at all to do with it. It was just there.

But to begin at the beginning: I was born at Mayday Hospital, Thornton Heath, on the 16th September 1945. My parents lived in Croydon then, but shortly afterwards

12

they moved to Coulsdon. My father was working for a car-hire company next to Beauman's bakery in Croydon and my mother as a nurse in Nethern Mental Hospital. One of my earliest memories of that time was almost my last. My elder brother, Barry, was aged about eight or so. I was aged about five. We were playing in an old Austin 8 that Dad had. He had it parked outside the house – on a hill. Not knowing what I was doing, I let the handbrake off. Beep! Beep! Away we went, Barry in the driving seat thinking he was the racing driver Fangio. As it happened, Dad was in the front garden talking to Eggie's Dad (Eggie was a friend of ours who always had egg down the front of his shirt – whatever he'd been eating). They came tearing after us, Eggie's Dad trying to get in one door, our Dad the other. They never caught up with us. We careered right on down the hill. Fortunately, at the bottom of the hill there was some wasteground belonging to the local farm. Some-how, through sheer good fortune rather than through good judgement of any kind, Barry managed to steer us onto it. We bounced over it, completely unaware of just how lucky we had been, and eventually came to a halt without actually hitting anything. Afterwards Dad gave me a clip around the ear. Barry got two whacks with the strap. And that was that. Finished. Done.

He was quite a small man, my father. But he was strong – and strong-willed. He needed to be both, I know, to cope with the pain he suffered from two duodenal ulcers which he had then. Quite often he would be in agony because of them. I remember that well too.

I liked Coulsdon. It was – and still is – quite rural. There were fields and farms all around us. Quite often Barry and I would leave the bungalow where we lived and go up to Farthing Down which overlooked the village. There was a little shop there which sold ice-cream. On our way up to the shop we'd nick potatoes and cabbages from the farms, whatever we could lay our hands on. God knows why.

13

Because they were there and because we could, I suppose. We were just kids. Kids do that sort of thing. Sometimes the farmers would chase us. Sometimes we wouldn't give them cause to; we would just sit on a gate or a fence and watch the cows going for milking or something. It was a good time. I remember it really fondly.

I was still only about five years old when we left Coulsdon and moved to Croydon. Grove Road. It was about 1951. My father had got a new job working for Ziggs & Chapman, a car-hire company near Croydon airport. Through that I got to sit in one of the very first Triumph Mayflowers – a horrible little car which had such square edges it looked as though it had been finished off with a trowel. A real honour that. My mother gave up working as a nurse and took up bar-work instead. Not only could she earn more by working as a barmaid, but she could also spend more time caring for my father, who was especially ill then, and for the latest addition to the family, Brian.

Some six months later and we were off again – to St. Augustine's Avenue, Croydon. Don't ask me why, but we moved house more often than an Arab moves tents when I was a kid. Always in the Croydon area. I found it a bit of a wrench moving from Coulsdon at first, but I soon got over it. I had a fantastic childhood in Croydon.

St. Augustine's Avenue wasn't far from the local bus station, on one side of which was Purley Oaks Junior School and on the other South Croydon Secondary Modern. I never had far to go to school; I went to both. I don't remember much about my time at Purley Oaks except that for two years running I was captain of the school cricket team. I loved that. One of my best friends from my days at Purley Oaks was John Austin. He and I were in the 18th Croydon Cubs together. I remember that when the time came for us to take the 11-Plus exams in 1957 we both bunked off; if you passed you wouldn't go to South Croydon Secondary Modern. We didn't want to take the

14

risk. Not that we thought we had a chance of passing anyway. So off we went to the chip shop. Playing truant like that is part of growing up in my opinion. It's not the crime some people like to make out it is.

Another lesson in growing up was learning that we'd have to resit the exams anyway. That was bad news.

We sat the exam second time around. The good news was: we failed. We went to South Croydon Secondary Modern.

The school was quite sports orientated and that suited me right down to the ground. Barry was already there, of course, and because he was so good at sports, he gave me something to aim at too. I wanted to be like him. Cricket, cross-country, football: you name it, he was first-rate at it. Sickening. He was much bigger than me. Good though I eventually got to be at cricket, cross-country, football, whatever, I never quite reached the standards I should have done; my size – or, rather, lack of it – was a real handicap. As I said in the preceding chapter, no matter how good I was, I was never going to be that good simply because I was so small. It was really irritating.

It had other drawbacks too. An area of Croydon renowned for being a bit rough was Waddon. You didn't get involved with Waddon boys if you could avoid it; given half a chance they would beat you to a pulp. They were horrible. Unfortunately, South Croydon Secondary Modern took Waddon boys so there was no avoiding them. Inevitably, I took quite a lot of stick from them in my first few years there – and from others – and for a while I felt rather overwhelmed by it all. I didn't like it. Who would? When he could, Barry looked out for me, of course, and in that respect I suppose I was quite lucky; if someone needed sorting out, he'd do it. It was quite handy having a big brother to threaten people with.

But when Barry wasn't around, I had to look after myself. Accordingly, I eventually gained something of a reputation for fighting – never mind that more often than not I wasn't to blame for starting any fights I got involved in. The thing was, I was determined not to be seen as an underdog, someone to be kicked around. I didn't want to be like that. So I started belting people back if they belted me. And sometimes even if they didn't . . . just in case.

I made a lot of friends at school. I can still see them vividly even though I haven't seen most of them for over thirty years. As with John Austin, we went to clubs together. We were in the Scouts together. We fought one another (I even got into fights with people I liked). We climbed up telegraph poles, nicked the bulbs out of street-lights, went onto building sites and wrecked them together. We had a great time. It was fabulous. We were really close. Quite often I would turn up at home after school with maybe ten or twelve of them in tow. I drove my mother mad. Haven't they all got homes to go to?

On Bonfire Night, mind, everyone came round to our house. It really was a big occasion in our family. Not only was it also Barry's birthday (same as Lester Piggott), but we had fireworks galore. Hundreds of them. My great-aunt, Marjorie Prior, worked in a fireworks factory and she got hold of rejects for us. They weren't dodgy or dangerous or anything like that; we weren't about to wipe St. Augustine's Avenue off the face of the map. It was just that some of them had fuses which were either slightly too long or too short, the rockets had damaged sticks. Things like that. It was better than Christmas we had so many. All of my friends would come round, neighbours, relatives . . . everyone. We'd have an enormous bonfire, an enormous guy (it collapsed the bonfire one year it was so heavy), the works.

My friends and I made off with a haul of bangers one year. We then got several lengths of metal pipe – plumbing pipe, that sort of thing – and stopped up the end of each of them. We would then light the bangers, drop them

16

down the other end, drop one or two stones in after them . . . and then take aim. Well, you can imagine; we smashed windows all over the shop. We had a whale of a time. Even though we were caught in the end, and I caught a hiding off my father, it was worth it. Those things were amazing. Whoosh! Another window gone! They were lethal.

Another homemade device which we got a lot of fun out of was a sort of skateboard: a plank of wood which we'd attach to a pair of skates. Off we'd go down the hills around where we lived. We'd hit cars, knock people over and scatter their shopping everywhere. We were terrible.

By now, our family's grown to seven. Barry, Brian and I have a sister, Mary, and another brother, Paul. We're like the Waltons. When Paul was born I think my parents decided that they'd better send Barry and me out to work. On Saturdays and during school holidays, I remember, Barry worked at Surrey Street market where some of our relatives had a stall. I ended up scraping dough off baking trays at Beauman's bakery. I was nine then.

When I was twelve or thirteen I had a Saturday/holiday job working on a stall at Surrey Street market. Bunny Jarman's it was called. It was a fruit and veg. stall. Bunny had been a family friend for years. I was amazed at the patter some of the stallholders there had, the way they tried to sell things. They were also snooker mad, most of them. And that's how I got into playing snooker. There was a snooker hall opposite the market and we'd all go in there. I all but needed the rest just to break, to clear the D, I was so small. But I soon learned how to play the game. And soon I was playing in matches – against kids from Streatham, Brixton, wherever. People would put money on us. Quite a lot of money too. I like to think that I made a lot of people very rich in that snooker hall. Barry came to play as well after a while. And, of course, he had to be better than me, didn't he? It was always the way. Soon he

17

was actually picking up winnings for himself. In fact, the jammy so-and-so was earning more in that snooker hall than he ever earned on the stall – and he was still working on that too from time to time. I'm glad I went there, I must say. I still enjoy playing snooker to this day. I have a game with quite a few of the jockeys whenever I can. Steve Smith-Eccles. Graham McCourt. Graham Bradley. Down here in Lambourn. Up in Newmarket. Wherever. It really is a good laugh. I also get to win money off them which is good.

At fifteen, Barry left school and went to work in a machine shop. Doing piece-work on a lathe. Dad wasn't at all pleased. But Barry just wanted to get out into the world · and get on with things, as it were. He had made his mind up. Barry has always been the 'wild' one in our family. He was drinking and smoking quite heavily even then. He had quite a few 'shady' friends too. Since then he's also gone on to be the biggest gambler in our family. He's a big fan of Lester Piggott (especially since they share the same birthday). He was straight back down the betting shop as soon as he made his comebacks. He loved that. Barry still lives in Croydon. He works in the building trade.

It was at fifteen, too, that Barry was getting into the Teddy Boy scene. I didn't want to be like him – or his mates – but I did like their clothes: the drainpipes (so tight that once you'd got them on you practically had to sleep in them), the quiffs, the d.a.'s. I was still in school uniform though. Worse, Mum was keeping me in short trousers! I was getting stick for that too. A short kid in short-trousers, it was no wonder that the Waddon boys tried it on.

But now, around 1960, I'm into long trousers at last, properly into my teens. I'm having a great time. At school I find I'm actually quite enjoying history, geography, art. It's only really maths I can't stand. I'm playing tennis, football, cricket, running cross-country, all the usual. I'm always doing something out of school too. One friend might be going swimming, so I'll go swimming. Someone else might be playing football, so I'll play football. There's always something going on.

Everything seemed to be happening then.

And then I got into bikes and girls.

Mum and Dad were brilliant. None of us kids ever really wanted for anything. They gave us everything they could. But I wanted a bike. Lots of my friends were getting them. I wanted one. And I wanted one of my own. I didn't want Barry's clapped-out thing. I wanted one of my own.

And then I got one. On the drip. From Geoffrey Butler Cycles. They made the frame especially for me. The bikes in the shop were just too big for me. It was a good bike I ended up with. It was a metallic gold colour, sort of mottled. It cost about £38. That was a lot of money. To pay for it I took on two paper-rounds. One in the morning. One in the evening. I lost the morning round almost as soon as I'd started. I didn't always deliver all the papers. And I kept on being late. The evening round – delivering *The Evening Standard* – I kept for about six months. If anybody failed to give me a Christmas box that year, I tossed their paper over a wall. I was only earning about 7s 6d a week. My dad made that up to 10s and that was what I paid weekly on the bike.

Apart from the fact that so many of my friends had one, another reason for me wanting a bike was that I was in love with a girl who was in the school athletic team. She had a bike and I could never catch up with her. But once I got the bike . . . Well, actually, I forgot all about her once I got the bike.

In truth, I wasn't that bothered about girls then. All that swapping spit when you were kissing. Ugh! Not for me, I thought – I'll shoot off for a bike ride. My sexual activities were pretty well limited to some furtive gropings. In the summer, like everyone else I was friendly with them, I'd bribe the girls with Lubbly Jubblies – those cartons of iced orange juice which were all the rage then and which Del from that lovely programme *Only Fools and Horses* is often referring to. From there, I'm sorry to say, I simply progressed – if that's the right word – to simply being a hit-and-run merchant. I'm afraid I was a dirty little devil. Whey-hay! And I'm gone. I often got a slap around the head for my trouble. And, of course, I no doubt deserved it. The teachers told me I was turning into a dirty little man. Thank goodness that was only a brief phase I went through.

So there I was doing my paper round, paying off my 10s a week at Geoffrey Butler's. And it was there that I began to meet all of these cycling enthusiasts. They would be in the shop with all the gear – the coloured vests, the shorts, the shoes. Finally, one of them asked me if I would be interested in joining their club, the West Croydon Wheelers.

I joined.

Quite regularly, on a Sunday, I would go on rides with the West Croydon Wheelers down to the South coast. Seaford. Hastings. Eastbourne. Places like that. Brighton. On other occasions we'd have time trials at, say, Crawley or Horley. I wasn't actually allowed to take part in the trials. Not to compete anyway. I was too young. Instead, then, I would often act as marshal. It was all really good fun. It was a fun little club.

And it was at about this time that I began to get to know Mary, the P.E. teacher at school. She was mainly involved with the girls' netball, hockey, athletic teams – things like that. But because the school teams, boys' and girls', used to travel together to compete with teams from other schools, she got involved with me too. And undoubtedly it was one of the best things that could have happened to me. As I've already said, she was so encouraging, so supportive. She was lovely. She laughed at me wanting to be in The Horse Guards, but she really did take the idea of me being a jockey seriously.

It must have rubbed off, because soon I did too.

I took her up on her invitation to go riding with her at her future father-in-law's in Banstead. As she said, I might as well find out whether or not I liked it at least.

Off I would go after school, cycle over to the house, muck out the horses and in return be taught how to ride. Mr. Bassett, Mary's father-in-law to be, had both horses and ponies and I got to ride both. Mary rode with me. She put me on lead reins, on a lunge rein when I rode in the paddock. She put me over jumps on a lunge rein at a nearby riding school. I fell off plenty of times and I got God knows how many saddle sores, but before long I was riding quite well. Not badly anyway. I liked it. I really liked it. Things were looking up. Perhaps I could make it as a jockey?

Of course, all of this took up a lot of my time and, inevitably, I gradually began to see less and less of my friends. I didn't like that. I missed seeing them. We were all just getting into clothes and partying then. Me especially. John Austin, Steve West (who is one friend I have kept in touch with from those days; he's in antiques now), Colin Fluter: they would all be asking me what I would be wearing next. *It'll be something different again, eh, Rod?* All of which was quite a turn up for the books; until then I'd been a scruffy kid, no two ways about it. I could never keep anything clean. Even my burning ambition to join The Horse Guards hadn't caused me to smarten up any.

Anyway, once I got into the riding in a serious way, that was more or less it. We seemed to go off in different directions. No more football, meeting up at The Olive Tree, the cafe we used to go to all the time . . . none of that. I had important work to do.

Like preparing for gymkhanas.

Yes, Mary persuaded me to compete in gymkhanas. And, yes, I did feel a prat about it at first. My friends thought that I was a prat too and said so. They thought it

21

was all cissy. The stick I took from them! It all highlighted the way things were changing, the fact that I wasn't really 'one of the lads' anymore. And when I told them I'd won a rosette! Imagine!

I didn't regret having done what I had though. Not a bit. I had even made new friends: the horses.

I remember that one of my first rides at a gymkhana (which were usually held at local farms) was on one of Mr. Bassett's horses named Ebony Rock. A black cob. And a bastard to ride. Everywhere that I wanted to go, it didn't. And vice versa. It was a disaster from the riding point of view – but I thoroughly enjoyed it. In fact, I couldn't get enough of riding the horses, these new-found friends of mine. I was that keen.

And then, through Mary, I learned that the racehorse trainer Cyril Mitchell (father of Philip Mitchell, who took up training in 1974 when Cyril retired) was looking for an apprentice jockey. Did I want the job? You can imagine my reaction. You bet I did. It was a fantastic opportunity and I leapt at it. Mr. Mitchell, who was based at Burgh Heath on the edge of the Epsom Downs, was quite prepared to hold the position open for me until I left school. But I didn't want to wait. I wanted to get started. I duly left school and set out to become a fully-fledged jockey. I was then not quite fifteen years old.

Suddenly the attitude of my friends changed. *Hey, is it true you're going to be a jockey?*

I don't know who was really the more surprised, me or them. But there it was: I was going to be a jockey.

Me. Little Rodney Simpson, a kid from Croydon.

APPRENTICED

Cyril Mitchell's yard at Burgh Heath was named Heath House. The stables were rust and white in colour, rustic . . . and built in an L-shape. I thought it was a fabulous place. When I first started as an apprentice I would cycle there. Every morning. I would get up in the early hours of the morning, cycle down to Croydon station, put the bike in the guards van, get off at Tadworth station, cycle to Burgh Heath. It was only when it was raining that I wouldn't do the journey like that. When it was raining my father would get the car out, drive me over. He was really pleased about what I was doing, got quite a kick out of it. Even when it wasn't raining he would wake me up, see me off. I think he was almost as excited about me being an apprentice as I was. I have to say, he and my mother couldn't have been more supportive during my time at Cyril Mitchell's. They were brilliant.

It was 1960 when I became an apprentice at Heath House. The end of summer, the beginning of autumn. I was on a six week probationary period to begin with. But I soon proved myself a capable worker in the yard, I think. I belonged, fitted in. I liked that.

Which isn't to say that the stable staff there didn't give me a hard time. They did. Things can be pretty tough when you first get started in racing and it was no different for me. They waited for my six weeks probation to be over (lulling me into a false sense of security) – and then they went to work.

They were bastards.

There was a pub next door to the yard, The Wheatsheaf.

It was owned by Mr. Mitchell's father. People would walk over the heath to visit it, to visit the local shops. In doing so they had to walk past our barn at the end of which was an open hatch. Outside this hatch there was a length of rope with a tyre hanging from it. What did my Heath House colleagues do? They stripped me off, tied me to this tyre – my hands tied to my ankles, a target painted on my backside – and swung me out in front of everyone who came by. I would wriggle like crazy to swing back in again . . . and they would swing me straight back out again. If you had any inhibitions about being seen naked in public you soon lost them. You had to. In and out of this hatch I would swing, people pointing up at me and everything. God knows what I must have looked like. In between times they would simply shoot things at the target I had painted on me, whoop and cheer everytime they scored a bullseye.

As I say, they were bastards.

And that was just the start of it. Sometimes they would tie my tack in knots so that I would get into trouble with Mr. Mitchell or the head lad, Gordon Trivett. Gordon, now, ran that yard like a prison camp. He could pick you off with a feed bowl from the other side of the yard if he wanted to. *Whack!* It wasn't funny getting into bother with him. And I was always in bother with him because of things like that. On other occasions they would rub treacle into my hair, stick my head down the toilet and flush it, undo my girths so that I would fall off whatever horse I was riding. Some of the tricks they pulled on me I just can't repeat here. They were obscene.

Now you can't let all of this get to you. You just have to endure it. It's all part of your initiation, as it were. It's inevitable. Equally, though, you would be stupid not to have a spat about it every now and then to show that you're not soft. And I got my own back on them in kind. I tied their tack in knots, put shoe-polish in their sand-

24

wiches, saddle-soap in their tea. Things like that. They beat me up for it. Every time. Without fail. They knew it was me who had done it. Sometimes they just beat me up anyway.

But, eventually, of course, you're accepted. It ends.

For me, that really came about after about three months or so, after I'd moved into digs.

Life really changed a lot for me then. For the first three months of my apprenticeship, you see, I had been continuing to ride Mr. Bassett's horses as well as working for Mr. Mitchell. I would go over to Banstead whenever I had a spare evening or had a day off (which was once every three weeks). Again, if it wasn't raining, I would cycle there. If it was, Dad would give me a lift in the car. But Mr. Bassett wasn't only a big help in allowing me to continue to ride his horses; he was also a big help in that he continued to show such an interest in me. He wanted to see me get on, was always encouraging me, pushing me, as it were. He was terrific. And so was Mary, of course. She would often be at the house when I went there and she too was always encouraging me, pushing me, wanting to see me get on. It really was fabulous.

I missed my trips out to Banstead when I left home.

I missed home when I left home. The couple who I was lodging with in Burgh Heath were really pleasant; the wife (I can't remember her name for the life of me) would wake me up early in the morning, make me breakfast before I set off over the heath for work . . . but I was homesick. I missed my Mum. I missed my Dad. I missed my brothers, missed my sister Mary.

After a while Brian started to come and stay with me at weekends. That helped. He would come to the yard with me. He used to do odd-jobs there; fetching this and fetching that, carrying buckets of water, sweeping up. That was the start of Brian getting into racing. In time he would go on to become an apprentice with Staff Ingham – and

25

later still to work with me for the trainer Alec Kerr. He enjoyed working at Heath House. I more than enjoyed him being there with me.

Sometimes I went home at weekends. When I came back to Burgh Heath I always had a food parcel with me. As I've said, my parents were tremendously supportive of me when I began as an apprentice. I was paid 15 shillings a week plus a clothes allowance at Heath House, so they had to subsidise me to quite an extent. But all I had to do was pick up the phone and ask; they would help me out with whatever I needed. For instance, I might have needed a new jacket or a new pair of boots. My clothes allowance wouldn't have covered something like that. They had to stump up. And they did, no hesitation, no complaints. They wanted me to have everything I needed.

I got over my homesickness soon enough. And working at Heath House, being away from home, being in racing certainly helped me to grow up. It toughened me up – just as it would later do for Brian and after him Paul (who would go on to be an apprentice with Albert Davison). Looking back, I think that we had all had such a fabulous home life that, really, we were a bit soft. We needed toughening up. Racing did us the world of good in that respect.

I thoroughly enjoyed working at Heath House. I thoroughly enjoyed working for Mr. Mitchell. He had been a good jockey in his time and he knew what he wanted. I didn't enjoy taking orders though – from him, from Gordon Trivett, from anyone – and right from the word go I kept thinking to myself "Jesus, I can't wait for the day when I'm giving 'em instead of getting 'em!"

My favourite horse then was First Ace. I always rode him in his work. The first horse I ever rode out to exercise, I remember, was Jury Boy. Another horse I was extremely fond of was Supermarket. All three were good horses and won their share of races while I was at Heath House.

26

Riding out onto the heath with yearlings which had only just been broken was great fun. For them as well as us. We would hack around, ride figures of eight. We used to play cowboys and indians, split up into groups and charge one another, hide somewhere and then ambush one another. It was all part and parcel of the training programme. These horses were babies. You had to play with them. You wanted them to remember their early days in training with affection. It's something which I still believe in now. You have to allow young horses to play.

Of course, there were also horses in the yard for whom I felt little or no affection. One was a grey, Chincilla Grey. That animal could split an apple on top of your head with one kick if it wanted to. Pinpoint accuracy. Only it didn't aim for the top of my head usually. It kicked me black and blue that bastard. Torremolinos was another brute. Savage. He was always trying to eat me. And then there was Exorbitant . . .

Now here I should point out that I still wasn't a very good rider. I was better at looking after the horses than getting up on them. I still had a lot to learn. When I went home to visit my parents, I would play on this fact. I would arrive at the front door, pretend that I had injured my arm, my leg or whatever. I would trudge in looking really down-in-the-mouth and have my Mum switch on the telly for me, put my feet up on the stool, make my supper. It was heaven. She would wait on me hand and foot. Finally, she would come back into the room, see me with my hands behind my head, grinning from ear to ear, my supper all gone and twig what I had done. She always fell for it. Always.

And then along came Exorbitant. It was quite early on during my apprenticeship at Heath House that Mr. Mitchell sent me out to work this crazy bastard of a horse. Exorbitant was a difficult ride and I think Mr. Mitchell wanted to see if I could cope, see how good – or bad – I really was.

As it happened, he never really found out. I galloped a couple of furlongs with Exorbitant during which he never stopped bucking and swerving. Suddenly one of the reins snapped. He went to jump a fence and I was off. Broke both collar bones.

That night I went home, both arms tucked inside my jacket, looking really sorry for myself. My Mum took one look at me, said "Oh no, you're not catching me like that again", and whopped me round the head.

I won't forget Exorbitant in a hurry. I never pretended to have injured myself when I hadn't ever again.

On another occasion it was a donkey which dumped me. It was kept in this pasture behind the yard and all the stable staff would try to ride it. They never succeeded though; it would buck them off. Quite rightly, it would have none of it. And then I had a go. Would you believe it; I stayed on. The donkey had the last laugh though. It took off through an adjoining orchard. I caught a branch across my head and all but knocked my teeth out. Everyone was in stitches.

Life was like that with the stable staff once I properly became part of the set-up at Heath House. We had some good times together. We would go to The Wheatsheaf, play darts. That was good. None of us really drank alcohol. I drank coke. True. The Wheatsheaf might have been right next door to us but none of us were real drinkers – not like a lot of the lads in yards now are. We would have a round, a chat, a game of darts . . . then off. Back to work. That was how it was.

I was at Heath House for about two and a half years. I didn't ride as an apprentice for Mr. Mitchell at all during that time, I simply wasn't good enough. Eventually Mr. Mitchell told me as much. He took me aside one day and said "Look, you're never going to be a jockey; you're effing useless . . . but you'll make a good stable lad." I was shattered. That was it for me. It wasn't what I wanted, just to be a stable lad. I had more ambition than that. I discussed the situation with my parents, told them "If I can't be a jockey I don't want to be in racing anymore." They understood how I felt and, again, were tremendously supportive of me.

Shortly afterwards then, I left Heath House and despite the fact that it wasn't easy for my parents (who still had Brian, Mary and Paul there too) went back home again, all of my hopes dashed, my future looking extremely uncertain.

I felt terrible. It wasn't what I had expected from my apprenticeship at all. I had been brought back down to earth with a real bump.

And it hurt.

FUNKY FLIPPER

Having left Heath House, my ambitions of becoming a jockey completely shattered, I was back at square one. My career in racing seemed to be over almost as soon as it had begun. Brilliant.

But being back in Croydon did have its compensations. For a start I was back with my old friends again: John (Austin), Steve (West), Colin (Fluter) et al. It was 1963, I was eighteen years old and we were all getting into Mod. If there's a good time to be kicking my heels, as it were, wondering what to do with my life, this is it. We've all got rid of our pushbikes now and we're on to scooters. I got mine through a friend of my father's. I wanted it to be different from everyone else's – and it was. A Vespa 150, it really was the business. It was chrome from top to toe, had mirrors all over the shop. It was absolutely fantastic.

Every weekend the Mods would set off from Croydon some two hundred strong. Scooters everywhere. We would head down to Brighton, Worthing, Hayling Island. Anywhere on the south coast which took our fancy. On a few occasions we even went as far as Devon or Cornwall. It was chaos. We never went anywhere without causing chaos. We liked causing chaos, creating havoc. We would hold traffic up; stop in the middle of the high street to have a sandwich, to have a chat . . . just for the hell of it. If any of the car drivers complained we would then all start blasting the klaxon horns on our scooters. The racket we would make! I want one of those horns for my boat down in Cornwall now. I can relive some happy memories. We didn't give a toss. We were terrible. And all the while we were on the road we would be singing this song *Chugga-lugg*, I remember. The person who first started singing it actually acquired it as his nickname.

The *Vespa* did wonders for my image, but I have to admit that, for a while at least, I did have some trouble with the rest of the look. Trouble was, I was still so ******* small. I couldn't get anything to fit me. Nothing that mattered anyway. Quite often I simply had to make do with whatever I could get my hands on. For a serious Mod with a serious scooter that just wasn't on. It wasn't on at all. I used to take a fair bit of stick for this oversight. *Why are you wearing that? Why aren't you wearing this? ******* look at you!* It used to get up my nose. I soon decided that if ever I could afford it, I was going to have all my stuff made up for me. I wasn't going to be left out just because I was such a runt. It wasn't fair. I wasn't having it.

And then a stroke of luck. I got a job working in James Edgar's, a clothes shop in Croydon. Suddenly I'm not earning the pittance I was earning as an apprentice at Heath House; I'm earning a bit more than that . . . *and* I get discounts. I'm away. I get the suede shoes, the white socks, the Ben Sherman shirts. And, of course, I get the parka. On the back of it, in big white letters, I paint Funky Flipper. That's me now. Funky Flipper. Don't ask me what it meant. I've got no idea. Something to do with music, pinball, dolphins . . . no idea. But there it was.

And there I was. Really looking the part now. All dressed up . . . and with somewhere to go.

I had a fabulous time as a Mod.

I had my first proper girlfriends then too. I always had some 'chick' or other on the back of the Vespa. One girl-friend, I remember, looked like Marianne Faithful. Lots of the girls had that look then. I broke her ankle. On the way back from Redhill – which was where she lived and where I first met her – I tipped the Vespa over. My one and only accident on the scooter, I think. She was one of many

31

girlfriends I had then. I can't remember her name. Strangely enough though, about three years ago – at the time of writing – I got a letter with a Redhill postmark on it. There was no address on the letter and it wasn't signed. It said do you know you have a daughter? Just thought I'd let you know. Imagine. I was stunned at first. Then I felt annoyed. Really annoyed. If I really did have a daughter I didn't know about, I wanted to know. Eileen, my wife, was very understanding when I said I wanted to get to the bottom of it all. But what could I do, in fact? There was no way that I could get to the bottom of it all. I had nothing to go on. I thought perhaps there might be a follow-up. There never was. Nothing. I still can't help wondering if it was that particular girlfriend who sent it though. I still can't help wondering if there was any truth in the letter, whoever sent it.

We had some outrageous parties back then, to get back to business. We were always having them. And if we weren't, it was fatal to let us overhear if you were having one; we'd be round like a shot.

And then there were the drugs, of course. Uppers, downers, purple hearts. Someone had a girlfriend who worked in a chemists. We would paint up all the pills she got us, sell them, a few quid a go. And there were always plenty of takers. We even sold smarties on occasion. Crazy.

Croydon Bowling Alley saw a lot of us. That was one of our favourite haunts. Once someone rode their scooter straight through it, rode out through the emergency exit. It was amazing. Those scooters were just so manoeuvrable though. They weren't like motorbikes. Jump on one of those, open up the throttle and you would be on your back, instantly. Hop on your scooter, on the other hand, and you could be straight off. No trouble. Just like that.

Sometimes trouble was just what we wanted. The fights we had down at that bowling alley! We would throw the

My mother and father in 1947

Me with the Horse Guards, 1954

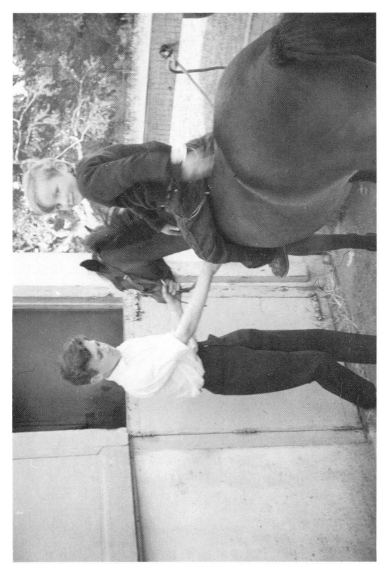

Mr. Bassett's stable c.1962 when I was apprenticed at Epsom to Mr. C. Mitchell

Me with Another Rondo, 1964 when I was with John Tilling

bowling balls at one another, run off down the alleys after the ones that got away. It was mayhem. It had to be seen to be believed.

Fabulous times. They really were.

I remember, too, when some of the boys began to swap their scooters for cars – Ford Consuls, Zodiacs, things like that – and their clothes began to get much more casual. For quite a while there was a craze for Bubblecars and those Messerschmitt contraptions where two of you would sit one behind the other in a sort of aeroplane cockpit on wheels with a steering wheel which was just like a joystick. Bubblecars had no reverse gear. A friend got stuck in a car park in his. We had to lift him out. On another occasion we lifted someone's Messerschmitt over a garden wall – while he was still in it.

Some of the things we did then were criminal acts. There's no denying it. But none of it was done with any malice. We reserved that for our occasional clashes with the Rockers. But even then the violence wasn't that bad – not like the media made out, like they still make out now. I never saw anyone left really badly injured or anything. We were all having fun. All of us. It was a laugh, that was all.

At the same time I was having a lot of fun at James Edgar's too. Though I say it myself, I was quite a salesman. I sold people stuff they had no intention of even looking at when they first came into the shop. It'll ride up with wear, Sir ... Your boy will look fabulous in this, Madam. The manager thought I was fantastic.

I can't remember the manager's name. I do remember that he grew the most incredible roses at his home in Wallington and that every day he would wear one of them in his lapel. He was always really smartly dressed and what with these roses in his lapel people were always coming into the shop just to compliment him on the fact. In any event, through him I learned that the shop's owner,

John Tilling, was really into horse racing. Not only that but he was a permit holder and trained a number of horses to run over the jumps. One was called James Edgar. Trained by Frank Muggeridge, it also ran on the flat. Now this was interesting news indeed to me. I was missing having horses in my life. I was missing them a hell of a lot. I knew that I couldn't be a jockey. That had gone, it was finished. Over. I knew. But I still wanted to be involved in racing somehow. I knew that too. It wasn't true that if I couldn't be a jockey I didn't want anything more to do with it anymore. Not now anyway. Now I did. I'd be a stable lad if I had to.

I begged and begged the manager to phone John Tilling up for me. I wanted to meet him. I wanted to see if I could go and work for him. I had been working in the shop for some six months then and I thought that it was time to move on, to start doing what I really wanted to do again. And that was to be involved in horse racing – at whatever level.

Eventually – probably because he was so sick of the way I was constantly pestering him and because he finally realised that I really was serious – he did so. He spoke to John Tilling about me.

A few days later my father drove me over to Worstead's Farm, East Grinstead, to keep the appointment with John Tilling that my manager had set up for me.

I was in luck.

John Tilling had a vacancy for a stable lad.

I got the job.

ALL GIRLS

Having been offered the job of stable lad at Worstead's Farm I left home for a second time. I found digs in East Grinstead at a place called Ashstead Wood. Unlike my previous digs, it was awful. My landlady was a big woman who always seemed to be wearing a pinny and carrying a mop. She was a monster. I had to pay extra just to have a bath and would have to ask her – very nicely – to turn the immersion heater on for me whenever I wanted one. It was terrible. And it didn't end there. I mentioned in the chapter before last that I didn't drink while I was at Heath House. Well I didn't drink while I was at Worstead's Farm either. But every time I came home late, which I admit was quite often, she would insist that I was drunk. She would rant and rave, threaten to tell Mr. Tilling, my parents, Uncle Tom Cobley and all. It was amazing. Eventually the friends I went nightclubbing with, Dennis McCarthy, the stable jockey, and some of the other stable lads, cottoned on to the fact that she was such a cow. They thought that it was dead funny and took to keeping me out late on purpose, just to land me in it. She, for her part, took to locking me out of the house. One night, then, arriving back there in the early hours again, I had to creep through the garden and shin in through a bathroom window she had left open. I didn't want to wake her up. I didn't want to wake her husband up. He worked for the council and quite often had to get up even earlier than I did. It was a tight squeeze – it was a top window – but I made it. The next morning when I went down to breakfast though there was a right atmosphere. I couldn't understand it. I hadn't made a sound climbing in through the window. James Bond couldn't have done better. What was the problem? I soon found out. "What time did you get in last night?" she asked me. I got home early, I said, went straight to bed because I was so tired. She wasn't having any of it. Every night she would make me cocoa before I went to bed. You can't go to bed without your cocoa! She laid into me something rotten. "You're a liar!" she said. "You didn't come home until four o'clock this morning!" She marched me off into the bathroom by my ear. There were muddy footprints everywhere. I had obviously got mud all over my shoes from the garden. There were two big bastards on the window-ledge, more in the bath, dozens of them all the way across the floor. The evidence was everywhere. "I let the dog out at half three," she went on. "And you weren't back then. And look at all this!" She nearly twisted my ear right off. And, of course, I got the usual. I'll tell Mr. Tilling! I'll tell your Mum and Dad! I'll tell, I'll tell, I'll tell!

One other thing I remember about my landlady is that she would never let me help myself to any biscuits from the biscuit barrel either. True. "Can I have a biscuit?" I would ask. "No!" "Just one." "No!" I'd look at her husband he'd be sitting there smirking, this look on his face that said "later, later". Sure enough, as soon as she left the room we'd help ourselves. Even he didn't dare help himself while she was around. As I said, she was a monster that woman. She really was. A monster.

Oh yes. And she used to put a warming pan in my bed, can you believe? She was probably hoping I'd get into bed one night, sit on it while it was still red hot. Crazy. It was a crazy place. I really didn't like it there in Ashstead Wood.

But I liked it at work. Mr. Tilling had a really good set up at Worstead's Farm. It was well laid out and the surrounding countryside was as pleasant as the yard itself. It had a good feeling about it. But what I really liked about it was the fact that the staff there were almost all girls. This is great, I thought, I've got a chance here. They're all girls *Girls!* I soon learned. Mardie, the Head Girl there at Worstead's Farm, who was only in her mid or late twenties, was tougher and stronger than any other stable Head I've met since. She was hard. Harder than Gordon Trivett even – and that's saying something. I made damned sure I never got on her wrong side whenever I could help it. She wouldn't only bite your head off, Mardie; she would spit it across the yard. She knew how she wanted that yard run and she got it. I learned more from her in the fifteen or so months that I was there than I think I've learned from anyone in such a short space of time. I learned more about how to run a yard and I learned more about horses. Much more. Mardie taught me about limbs, joints . . . a horse's conformation. I really can't overstate just how much I learned from her. I learned a lot. I got to be a really good stable lad at Worstead's Farm, though I say it myself. I worked hard. Not only because I was so pleased to be back in racing again, back working with the horses, but because I enjoyed it there so much. And it wasn't only Mardie who helped me get on then. There was Dennis McCarthy and his wife-to-be, Christine, too. They were really good to me while I was at Worstead's Farm. They soon became close friends who I could always turn to for advice – anything. They run a livery yard now. Their son, Tom, is a good amateur jockey.

On the other hand Dennis was also one of those friends from the yard who took such delight in keeping me out late and getting me into trouble with my landlady. And those weren't the only times he had a laugh at my expense, I have to say. Once, when I was leading up one of our best horses, The Master's Toy (winner of eight races in the 1962–63 season), at Plumpton, I met this girl. I asked her out. We went to the cinema. Dennis and some of the other lads were there too. Halfway through the film I tried getting my hand inside her shirt. I thought that that was what she wanted. Unfortunately she didn't and pow! she whacked me across the face just to make sure I got the message. Dennis and the rest of them loved it. She's smacked him in the kisser! Do it again! Nice one! I didn't know which was the more embarrassing, being slapped or having that lot sitting up behind me jeering about it.

At this time I was still a skinny little shrimp; a little over five feet tall, weighing just over seven stone. That small. And I still wasn't very strong either. Which meant, of course, that I kept getting run away with. I'd get run away with riding everyday exercise. I'd get run away with when we rode out on the gallops above Alfriston on the Sussex Downs (a really beautiful place, but absolutely freezing in winter; the wind!). I'd get run away with when we gave the horses a spin on the now sadly defunct Lewes racecourse where we occasionally worked them. I got run away with everywhere. Everywhere. The only horse I could control was The Master's Toy – probably because, like me, he was only small. Everything else would just take off with me, make me look a right prat. Mardie and the rest of the staff thought it was a great joke. There was this large paddock which we used to ride around at Worstead's Farm. As soon as we took the horses in there they'd say to me "Cheerio, see you when you're on the next circuit" – and sure enough I'd be off. As soon as I got into the paddock. Anything that pulled and that was it. Gone. I just couldn't hold strong horses, headstrong horses. Round and round that paddock we'd go, me hanging on for dear life knowing that there was absolutely nothing that I could do about it. It was terrible.

At which point I must mention Tom, the Tilling's gardener. He was a lovely man. Whenever things weren't going well for you he would always buck you up. Always. You could always talk to Tom. Everyone at Worstead's Farm loved him. He certainly made me feel better about being shown up by practically every horse in the yard. He listened to me complaining about it, made me laugh about it too.

But, of course, the problem wouldn't go away. I couldn't ignore it – much though I might have liked to.

Eventually I went to Mr. Tilling. "Look," I said. "I'm having real problems with these big jumpers here. You tell me to go round the field twice, I go round thirty two times. You tell me to go quietly up the road, I go up there flat out. I'm getting fed up. I can't manage them. They're all stronger than I am." I knew that he had horses with Frank Muggeridge who trained at Crabbett Park near Crawley and I asked if, perhaps, I could go there. I thought, hoped, that I might get on better with flat horses. It was the chasers who were taking off with me, that I couldn't control – big horses. Not only that, but I realised that if I did get on better with the flat horses then there might even be the possibility of my getting a ride in public there. Even if I only got one ride it would be worth it; at least one ambition fulfilled. Mr. Tilling though it was worth a try and promised to call Frank Muggeridge to enquire whether or not he could take me on, even it was only part time. He was really supportive, really helpful. He could just have told me to give up, but he didn't – whatever he might have thought privately. If there was a chance of me getting on, he wanted to help me do so. I couldn't have asked for more.

Once again I was in luck. Frank Muggeridge was looking for an apprentice. He phoned Mr. Tilling, said: "All right, we'll give the boy a chance, start him up full time."

I was about to begin my apprenticeship for a second time. Only this time around I had much more realistic expectations of what I might achieve. My feet were on the ground.

I had started work at Worstead's Farm in October 1962. I left to start work at Crabbett Park in January 1964.

A PACK OF JOKERS

Crabbett Park was even more pleasant than Worstead's Farm. It had a terrific atmosphere. It had an archway at its entrance with a clock on the top. The stable staff had to go up some stairs at the side to wind it up each evening. That was part of our job. We always overwound it. It was always telling the wrong time, ding-donging when it shouldn't have. Useless. The yard itself was quite old with open box fronts arranged around a central courtyard. It was really peaceful. It's a tragedy that it isn't a training establishment anymore but the M25, which now runs right by it, deprived it of its gallops, everything. It was devastated. It's an equestrian centre now, only a shadow of what it used to be.

Frank Muggeridge trained chasers and flat horses then. Quite a few of the horses ran under both codes. No doubt about it, he was a class trainer, Mr. Muggeridge. Trouble was, he just never really made a name for himself. I don't know why. He won a few decent races here and there but he never really won any of the big ones, end of story. He was a stout man, quite stern when he had to be, but he often turned a blind eye to some of the things we got up to in the yard – if they were done in fun. If there was any malice involved he'd stamp on you, hard. He didn't mind you having a bit of a laugh and a lark, but if it went too far . . . that was it. The end. It stopped. I'm not sure, but I think he had been quite a successful jockey in his time.

We had a lot of fun, I must say. It was a fabulous time. Every day of every week there was some mischief or other going on. Some mornings when you were out riding work you would suddenly find that your girths had been un-done. You'd look down and there would be nothing there. Nothing. Someone who was riding something which allowed them to take a liberty would have ridden up alongside you, simply pulled them loose. And they would usually do it when you were riding some unruly so-and-so who would be hard enough to sit on at the best of times. Opposite the yard there was a clapped-out old building where chickens were kept. We used to nick eggs from there . . . occasionally an old boiler. Back in the yard you were always having your stuff interfered with. Your sand-wiches, your clothes, your tack. There was always some-thing. Always. That was just the way things were.

I had only been there for a few weeks or so when some of the boys threw me into a corn bin, put the latch on it. The corn still had the shucks on it – it wasn't as well-prepared then as it is today – and it itched like crazy. I was effing and blinding, kicking, punching the sides of the thing. It was a bloody small box; I felt like I couldn't even breathe in there. I was going crazy. Mr. Muggeridge came along, asked what all the noise was about. When the boys let me out again he made me clean all of the bins in the yard. Me! What had I done wrong? That was the sort of man he was. He liked to join in the fun at times. He had a real sense of humour. He was all right.

I really enjoyed myself with Mr. Muggeridge. I can't tell you how much. The horses weren't exceptional by any means (which was certainly one reason why Frank Mug-geridge didn't gain the reputation he deserved), but the people who worked there were. No two ways about it. They were brilliant. We got to be really close there, all of us. Perhaps Frank Muggeridge didn't gain the reputation he deserved simply because we were such a bunch of bastards; spending too much of our time having a good time. There were some charcoal burners near Crabbett Park. Sometimes when we took the horses out we would just take them as far as the burners and then come straight back again. One day we found an old car there, a Riley. It was the real McCoy too; running-boards along the sides, a spare on the back. What did we do? We nicked it; six or seven of us, drove it off and, after tearing up and down the road in it several times, crashed it into a tree. I say into. In fact, it ended up the tree. Like it was trying to climb it or something. It was practically upright. And we were all still inside it, laughing our heads off. Anyway, we all fell out, pulled it down from the tree and then legged it again. We later learned that the car belonged to one of Mr Muggeridge's owners. He had left it by the burners while waiting for someone to buy it! We never owned up. When it was finally brought into the yard it was in a hell of a state . . .

I was nineteen when I started at Crabbett Park. Looked much younger, of course. I had moved out of those horrible digs at Ashstead Wood, left that monster of a landlady behind me, and had moved back home with my parents – again. It was the obvious thing to do. Crawley was just down the road from Croydon, straight down the A23, the Brighton Road. Easy. I shot down there on my scooter. And I must say, that was even more the business by now. More mirrors, More lights. More everything. Fantastic! I was up at five every morning, back again at eight. I had a girlfriend back in Croydon by then too, so that was another good reason for going back there.

My Mum used to do all my washing for me – of course. One evening Barnie sneaked round to my scooter which I used to leave at the back of the yard, wrapped up a dead rat in some dirty clothes I was taking back home. My Mum put the whole lot straight into the machine. When she went to get it all out again she had a fit. The smell! The mess!

Another amusing incident I remember involved a scarecrow. One evening a few of us went to a local pub. I still didn't drink then so, along with some of the others, I left early. On the way back to the yard we saw what looked like a body lying in some bushes. It was this scarecrow. Knowing that one of the other lads who had had quite a lot to drink was following on behind us, we decided to play a joke on him. We hung this scarecrow from the branch of a tree so that it looked like someone standing in the road. Then we went and hid. Sure enough, along comes our drunk, weaving all over the shop. As soon as he saw the scarecrow he started shouting at it, challenged it to a fight. And in he went, fists flying. The scarecrow was swinging backwards and forwards, bumping into him. The rest of us were in stitches. But the best was yet to come. The next day our scarecrow-basher starts telling us how he was attacked on the way home by a gang. Not only that; they were armed with bottles and knives! We didn't tell him for weeks that it was us who had set him up.

Less amusing was the stick some of the lads gave me and a girl I was going out with then. I had met Penny at Crawley Bowling Alley, the scene of so much fun during my days as a Mod, of course. She was black. They gave us a really hard time. They were terrible. Really terrible. They gave us stick something rotten. I didn't like it at all. In the end we had to split up because of it. It was that bad. We were on the bus once, I remember, and they were shouting all these remarks at us. Stupid. It wasn't funny. And I have to say it wasn't easy having a girlfriend then at the best of times. You never had any money. You were always broke. I was reading a while ago about some Russian lorry driver who was only earning £3.70 a month. I thought, I know how that feels! I've been there!

The high point of my time at Crabbett Park was having my first ride in public. My riding had improved quite a bit by then (the summer of 1964); I was getting on better with the flat horses Mr. Muggeridge trained – even if some of the chasers he had still tended to run away with me on occasion. I may still have been knee-high to a grasshopper and weighed on 7st 4lb (which, in fact, was quite heavy for an apprentice jockey of my age), but I was getting stronger. It made all the difference. Anyway, one of the owners, Bill Meadon, a manager for Crockford's, a casino chain based in London, put me up for a ride on his horse. Ramillies, it was called. It was entered up for a little race, a three runner stayer's handicap at Folkestone where it was due to carry 6st 7lb. The minimum weight then was 6st 7lb. I had 11lb to lose.

Getting that weight off nearly killed me.

First of all, of course, I stopped eating and drinking. I ran. I sucked lemons. I had mustard baths. It wasn't enough. I got buried in the muck heap to sweat more off. You have to be keen for a ride to go along with the idea of sitting like that for a few hours, up to your neck in horse shit. But I was. So I did. We didn't have the luxury of saunas then.

Still I hadn't lost enough weight.

Onto the laxatives.

Now in those days shiny wellington boots were the norm. They were part of the uniform. Everyone wore them. Everywhere. All the time. That's why I've got bunions today; I used to wear those bastards all of the time and they drew your feet something rotten. One day a crowd of us went into Crawley for the afternoon. Usually when we went there it would be to make nuisances of ourselves. We would order too many cream teas in a cafe we went to. We would dress up in all sorts of stupid things in the clothes stores. We would chat up all the women behind the counters. It was all just good crack, good fun. On this particular occasion someone went and nicked something or other. We ended up getting chased through a music store. Nobber and I ran full tilt into, of all things, a drum kit. The noise! It was like the Keystone Cops. It was absolute chaos.

So we've made our escape all the same, and now we're sitting on the top of a bus on our way back to Crabbett. Park. And this is where the laxatives come in. The boys had only gone and put some in my tea. I didn't know anything about it. But if that wasn't bad enough, they had gone and overdone it a bit. Suddenly they start to work on me. My guts starts to pinch. "Jesus," I said to them. "I've got the trots!" It was then that they told me what they'd done. They thought it was a great joke. I was in agony. It was no joke to me. There was nothing I could do about it – it was down the wellies, the lot. I squelched my way back to the yard all my pride having gone straight out of the window, nowhere to be seen. I mean, when you're in that state you just can't hold your head up at all, can you? It's gone. They didn't let up at all. Mind you, if it had been the other way round I probably wouldn't have done either.

Finally, though I'm down to 6st 7lb. I'm off to Folkestone to ride Ramillies. I'm really excited. This is it, I'm thinking. This is what I've been waiting for. Dennis gave me plenty of advice. So did Mr. Muggeridge. And so did everyone else in the yard. When I was getting changed in the wooden shack which served as a changing room at the course, I got more. This time from the two jockeys I was up against: none other than Geoff Lewis and Joe Mercer. Two of the best jockeys at that time. "Just go out there and enjoy yourself," they said. "But don't get in our way!"

I took Ramillies down to post really steadily, following Mr. Muggeridge's orders. He was a strong horse, Ramillies, and if I hadn't he would have run away with me. I wasn't having that happening in public. No way. I kept him on a tight rein, kept his head hung over the rails. Folkestone had metal rails in those days (which, thankfully, aren't there now) and all the way down to the start, which was about a furlong from the grandstand, his nose was going *bonk, bonk, bonk* against them. I can still hear it now. It was like when you were a kid, running a ruler along railings. The same sort of sound.

Once at the start, Geoff and Joe started on at me again, telling me not to get under their feet during the race. There were no stalls in those days, of course, so we lined up – and I jumped off in front. My instructions for the race itself were to go off fast, make all. Coming round into the home straight I'm still there. Behind me Geoff and Joe are shouting all sorts at me. Get out of the way, you little bastard! Lay over! The sort of thing you always get in a race. They soon got to me. Geoff was on Touroy, the favourite. He won it by one and a half lengths from Joe's mount, Sherry Netherland. I finished eight lengths further back. Third. Last.

That was it for me, after that race. I didn't want to be a jockey anymore. That one race had made up my mind for me. That was my lot. It was too hard, too tough. I hadn't realised just how much I was going to have to punish my body just for that brief moment of 'glory'. I could at least say that I had done it, that I had had a ride in public as a proper jockey, but that was it. No more. For days, weeks, afterwards I just couldn't eat or drink properly again. My body just couldn't readjust. It wasn't having it. Ease up, it was saying; we haven't done this for ages. I started producing crystals in my water. I was quite ill, in fact. What I had done was to shrink a kidney. That's what happens when you waste: you literally shrink your gut. Because of that experience, though, I really do appreciate now just what jockeys have to go through to keep their weight down. I can relate to it. They may not get buried in the muck heap anymore, but they still have to starve themselves, sweat the weight off somehow . . . use laxatives. It's not at all easy. It hurts. It's a constant struggle. Quite a few jockeys regularly have to regurgitate their food, it's true. That's how bad it can get. Terrible.

So that ride on Ramillies was definitely a turning point

for me. I had got to where I wanted to go, discovered that I didn't like it. Now where? I carried on working at Crabbett Park for about a year and, in fact, I had another four rides. One was on Ramillies again, at Brighton. We finished nowhere. After that I had another two rides at Brighton, both on a horse called Midnight Star. We finished nowhere on our first visit. But on our next we came second. That was quite an exciting race. It's an interesting track to ride, Brighton. You'd think, looking at it from the stands, that it's shaped like a horseshoe, but it isn't; it's more like an S-shape. You really have to manoeuvre for position going around there. And then, of course, there's the fact that it's a real switchback track too; up and down all the way. I enjoyed my rides there. My final ride was on a horse called Game Duchess at Epsom, a similar switchback track. She was quite a good filly, Game Duchess, but prone to injury. We came nowhere. I only kept my licence for that one season.

All the while I gave the question of just what I was going to do next a lot of thought. That was what was most important to me now. And then, during the summer of 1965, it just so happened that some big changes started to take place at Crabbett Park. A lot of the old horses left to go to other yards or because they were being retired. Mr. Muggeridge was thinking of moving to another yard. I decided that it was time for me to move on too. It seemed like a good idea. I had spent some sixteen months there and I couldn't have enjoyed it more. But all good things have to come to an end. I wanted to learn more about horses. That was my ambition now. I wanted to learn everything I could. Everything. I knew that it was time for the pranks, all the messing about to end. I wanted to get on. I was beginning to think more and more about doing some training myself at some point in the future. Why not? Even if I couldn't train I wanted to be better at the job I was doing. I didn't just want to be a stable lad doing my three; I had to have more of a sense of purpose than that. More of a sense of direction.

Eventually, through connections I had made while riding out on the Sussex Downs (for both Mr. Tilling and Mr. Muggeridge), I learned that John Hooton, a trainer based at Wilmington, near Polegate in Sussex, was looking for staff. He had a well-established reputation as a veterinary surgeon as well as a trainer. With my poor academic record I was never going to be able to get into veterinary college or anything like that (it would have been like trying to join The Horse Guards all over again), but all of this was something I definitely wanted to know about. John Hooton, I decided, was the man for me. So, I gave him a call, arranged an interview with him. He offered me a job.

It was done. I was on my way again.

To Sussex.

ON THE MOVE

You couldn't really imagine John Hooton as a racehorse trainer. As a vet, yes. But not as a trainer. He was a star. He was a really likeable man.

I wasn't at Wilmington very long; I went there in October 1965, left the following March. But I learned a lot during those few months. I learned about blood-tests, firing, pin-firing. I learned about most of the operations horses undergo, in fact. It was fascinating. I often assisted in the operations; shackling the horses up, applying anaesthetics ... standing by with the swab. Things were much more serious at John Hooton's. That was the atmosphere there. It was good. It encouraged you to learn, to take things in. It was just what I needed. It did me a lot of good.

Of course, working all the way down there in Sussex meant that I had to move into digs again. So I moved into, of all things, a tea-shop. My landlady was very pleasant but she had so many cats. The place was overrun with them. They were everywhere. They drove me mad. I used to open the windows sometimes, let them out hoping that some of them would never come back again. I hated them. The irony is I'm now married to someone who loves them. Once again I'm surrounded by cats.

I was going out with a girl, who I had originally met during my time at Worstead's Farm, while I was at John Hooton's. She lived in East Grinstead. I'd sold the Vespa by then so I didn't have any transport. If I'd been over there for the evening, then (or if I had been home for the weekend), I would thumb a lift back to Wilmington. If I couldn't get a lift I would walk. If I left her house at midnight on such occasions I might still be walking at two, three in the morning. Crazy. Sometimes I'd stop and have a kip in a phone box. More often though, I'd make my way to a railway signal-box which was situated near the yard, next to a level-crossing. I'd get there at three or four. The signalman would let me in and I'd kip by his stove. He'd wake me up at six when it was time for me to go to work.

Brian joined me at John Hooton's for a while. I liked that. It was like being back at Heath House again having him around. He was still keen to get into racing if he could, so along he came. He learned to ride at Wilmington.

If there's one thing, I can't say I miss looking back at my time at Wilmington, it was going out on the gallops above Jevington and Alfriston on winter mornings. I'd been there during my time at Worstead's Farm, of course, and although, as I've already said, that particular part of Sussex is really beautiful . . . when you get a cold wind coming over there! When I was riding Mr. Hooton's horses work on the gallops I often found myself wondering why I'd gone back, why I hadn't learned my lesson. It was freezing!

Anyway, after about five months I was on the move again. Barnie, who had left Crabbett Park shortly after me, had moved to Alec Kerr's yard at Holmwood, near Dorking. In fact, quite a few of the lads who used to be at Crabbett Park had gone there. Barnie told me that there was a job going, did I fancy it? In fact, he said, they're desperate for staff, bring your brother too if you want. So off we went. My parents were pleased that Brian was staying with me; I could show him the ropes, look after him. Brian was just pleased that he'd got his first full-time job in racing. I was pleased that I was moving on again, that things were happening.

Alec Kerr trained flat horses mostly, but he also had a few chasers. A 'gentleman' trainer of the old school, he

54

had been training for years. He had had to ride horses to the races in his time; camping them overnight, riding them on again the following morning. He was easy-going. Too easy-going, in fact. He wasn't anywhere near as hard as he could – should – have been on his staff. But he was a good trainer, especially good at placing his horses, I remember. His yard, however – Rosewood Cottage, it was called – was a mess. A more dilapidated place you could not imagine. It wasn't his fault; it was just falling apart. And to make matters worse the Dorking–Worthing road ran right alongside it. We all made the best of things though. Tony Dennis was the Head Lad and stable jockey. Pat Mitchell, who is now training at Newmarket, was there. Together with the boys from Crabbett Park we made a good team. Everything seemed to come together quite well. As far as I was concerned, it was good to settle down into the routine of being a stable lad again. My time with John Hooton had been a time of readjustment for me, a transitional period. Now was the time to push ahead in a new direction – towards eventually becoming a trainer myself. Which wasn't to say that I didn't continue to have a laugh at Holmwood when the opportunity arose. I did.

During the winter we went skating on a nearby pond. Not in skates. In our wellies. You should have seen us. And then we would get a big rope. One of us would stand in the middle while the rest of us hung onto the end. The person in the middle would start spinning us around – faster and faster and faster. Round and round this frozen-up pond we'd go. And then the person in the middle would let go of the rope. We would shoot off everywhere. Slide across the ice on our faces. Crash into the surrounding undergrowth. Crash into each other. It was chaos. Brilliant fun.

I had been at Holmwood a little over two years when Mr. Kerr finally got the chance to move to a new yard. A number of his owners (principally a Mr. Foden who I think I'm right in saying was involved with the refuse lorry manufacturers Drinkwaters) bought a yard at Coldharbour for him. Crocker's Farm it was called. I had worked hard at Holmwood and he acknowledged the fact by making me Travelling Head Lad once the move to Crocker's Farm was completed. It was fantastic. I was really pleased. It was proof that I really was getting somewhere, moving on, moving up. To reflect my new-found status I went out and bought a car: a Sunbeam Imp. Brand spanking new. It had none of the style of the Vespa, (it had the engine in the boot, for God's sake) but at least it got me to where I wanted to go ... and I didn't get a soaking if it rained. It was my pride and joy. My parents, already pleased by the fact that Brian had joined me, were especially pleased by my getting the job as Travelling Head Lad. They had been a little worried when I had given up my ambitions to become a jockey. Now they could see that I was making progress towards fulfilling another. As it happened, they were going up in the world themselves then. It was at about this time that they moved house again; this time to Saunderstead – which was, and still is, quite an upmarket area of Croydon. I felt quite pleased for them too. We (my brothers, Mary and me) all felt as though we'd won the football pools or something when they said they were moving there. All our noses flew up in the air.

I was still quite young to hold a position like Travelling Head Lad and I had to work hard to earn the respect of the staff. That's one of the things I remember most from my time at Coldharbour. I had to be quite hard. I knew I couldn't allow anyone to take any liberties. If they did I whopped them. If I hadn't they would have walked all over me. That was one of the important lessons I had learned from Mardie. It's like marking someone in a football match. Early on you have to get a hard tackle in, let them know you're there, that you mean business. That's how I was. I let people know that I was serious; I was going to do my job properly – whatever I might have got up to in the past. I meant business.

It is an important job being Travelling Head Lad. You have to take care of the horses, of course, see to their feed, their water, their tack. You have to see to the staff travelling to the course with you. You have to meet the owners. Basically, what you're doing is taking the strain off the trainer as much as you possibly can. It's hard, but it's interesting too. You get to learn about all the courses. You get to go abroad if you're lucky. And I was. I went to Ireland. To Phoenix Park, the Curragh, Roscommon. I went to France on a number of occasions too. Sometimes by air, but more usually by ferry. It was fantastic. You also learned how many wristwatches you could get around one horse's leg and then cover with a bandage, how many bottles of perfume you could get in the hay-net without them rattling. It was bloody good fun. It really was.

The horse that I travelled abroad with most was called Joshua, 33–1 fifth to Nijinsky, Yellow God, Roi Soleil and Amber Rama in the 1970 Two Thousand Guineas. And that was a good Two Thousand Guineas too. There have been few better. Joshua might have finished even closer but for the fact that Mr. Kerr got so involved with winning the race that he got the horse ready a shade too soon. He was undoubtedly the best horse in the yard. Lester Piggott rode him in the Prix Musador in France. And he won. But some of the trips we made! I remember flying to France from Bristol once. How that rattling old crate we went in ever got off the ground I don't know. I was terrified. Travelling wasn't anywhere near as comfortable then as it is now. You often had to rough it.

Percentage-wise, Alec Kerr was one of the best trainers in the country at that time. He only had between twenty and thirty horses but he always managed to notch up about twenty winners. He had a good relationship with

Geoffrey Rickman (brother of the television commentator, John) who owned a stud at Bookham and he used to get some really decent horses from him. Almost all of them would turn out to be good winners. Basically, it was a case of buying up good horses and then giving them a really good training. He was good at both. I learned a lot from Mr. Kerr. A lot that I was going to be able to put into practice later on – just as I was already putting into practice things that I had learned from Mardie years earlier.

A low point during my time at Coldharbour with Alec Kerr concerned my youngest brother, Paul, who had developed into a useful jockey. He was getting quite a few rides. And then, riding in a race at Sandown one afternoon, he was involved in a bad pile-up. He took an horrific fall, fractured his skull amongst other things. The jockey Brian Jago broke his leg really badly in the same accident. He was out of racing for a long, long time. And so was Paul, of course. But to make matters worse he was then involved in a hit-and-run accident. He was left in a coma. He recovered . . . but it was obvious that he was never going to ride again. The combination of the two accidents had left him really badly affected. He works for me now. Once it was Brian who worked with me, now it's Paul. It's good having someone from the family so close at hand. He's someone I can turn to when I can't really turn to anyone else. But, as I say, that accident that he had at Sandown marked a real low point during my time at Coldharbour. It was a real low point for the whole family. For a long, long time we were all very worried about Paul.

What I didn't then know was that there was another low point about to overtake me. Just when things seemed to be going so well for me I too was about to have an accident which would change my whole life.

A BAD BREAK

Ever since I can remember I've been football crazy. I've always liked a bit of a kick-around whenever I can. I've always been a Crystal Palace supporter. And while I was at Alec Kerr's I got involved with a football team. Windmill Wanderers F.C. we were called. But don't get the idea that our team was made up of five foot nothing jockeys and stable lads, vulnerable to crosses and high balls; it was made up of my mates from around Croydon and Purley, that area. Brian played. He was a fantastic centre half. My sister Mary was engaged to Mick, a plasterer from Bookham, then. He played too. We were quite a good little team. We bought our own colours (sky blue, sponsored by the local pubs, including *The Railway* at Purley, our local), joined the District League in the 1970–1 season and finished second.

But I didn't finish the season. We were playing in the mud one Sunday when I got tackled from behind. It was an accident; the guy just came clattering into me largely because he couldn't stop himself. Four compound fractures between the knee and the ankle of my left leg. That's what I got. I didn't hear a thing, but everyone else on the pitch said they heard it go. Brian still talks about it now. He hardly ever talks about the winners I've had, but he talks about that. The bottom of my leg was left flapping over my knee. It was that bad. It was horrific. I was in agony. I was chewing the grass, screaming. I got taken off to Redhill General. "Chop it off!" I'm shouting. "Just chop the thing off!" I got into the hospital at about five o'clock. Just my luck; there weren't any surgeons there to see to

59

me. The doctors who did have a look at my leg said: it's gone. It was frightening. I didn't really want my leg chopped off. Jesus! In the end they decided to strap me up, leave things until a surgeon could have a look at me. They put me out, put my leg in this plastic-bag affair, left me overnight.

The following morning: a stroke of luck, if you can say that you can have any luck in such a situation; Dr. Ring, a surgeon who specialised in hip-replacements was in the hospital, checking on some of the patients he had operated on during the week. He came to see me, sent me straight off to the operating theatre. He thought he could save my leg, mess though it was, plated it up for me.

After the operation I was put in a hip-spiker for a month. This was a plaster-case that covered my whole leg and came right up around my waist. It immobilised my leg completely. But just to make doubly sure that I couldn't move, I was also put in traction.

The weeks dragged by. I was depressed. It was touch and go whether I would ever be able to walk again, never mind ride or play football. Depressed? I was devastated, kept thinking the worst, that the leg might still have to come off. I felt really sorry for myself. Finally, though, I was taken off traction. The hip-spiker went. I was sent back home. The whole of my leg was still in plaster though. I was still helpless. I was like that for three months. I drove my parents mad. I couldn't do anything for myself. If they took me out anywhere they had to lie me out on the back seat of the car. It was a terrible time.

What I didn't know was that things were going to get worse. Much worse.

Back I went to the hospital. They took the plaster off to see what was happening. Nothing. Nothing was happening. The leg just hadn't healed; the bones hadn't knitted together properly. Even with the plates in there it just wasn't happening. Having so many fractures so close together was really bad news, that was the problem. The doctors decided to put me back in plaster, give it another two months. They did allow me to start using crutches though, so at least I felt I had made some progress. For the next two months I was in and out of hospital: getting my hopes up, being disappointed, getting my hopes up, being disappointed. When the two months were up I was sent back into the operating theatre for another operation; still the bones weren't knitting back together. I had some of my fibula removed, used as a graft around the plates. I was sent back home again. That meant being back in plaster for another four months. I tried to put all this time to good use though. Building on my experience from John Hooton's, I started studying veterinary science again, took a veterinary college entrance exam. And I passed. I then aimed a little higher, took a University entrance exam for a veterinary course. I failed that. It wasn't that I didn't know about hobdaying, haematology, using anaesthetics. I just couldn't spell them!

Fourteen months after the accident I was only in plaster from my knee down. I was getting around on the crutches quite well. But still it wasn't the end. Not by a long chalk.

Into hospital I went for the operation to remove the plates. They took the plaster cast off me . . . and half of my calf muscle came away with it. It had been in the plaster so long that it had actually grown attached to it. My whole leg was a mess, in fact. I'd lost several inches off my thigh muscle just through not being able to use it properly. Truth be told, if I had been a horse, I would have been put down. Shot.

Another spate of operations followed. I had the plates taken out of my leg. I had another plaster put on. I was quite a regular at Redhill General by then, had quite a few mates there. We all kept our spirits up by bucking the system a bit. Some evenings we would order taxis, get the drivers to pick up takeaways for us, deliver them through a window on our ward having told them exactly where we were. And we were always smoking at night too. We'd have huge cigars, keep all the windows open to let the smoke out. We were like schoolboys. The rest of the time we would sit in the conservatory at the end of the ward, watch telly, play cards. There was a good atmosphere there (when it wasn't full of cigar smoke) and it helped a lot. Anyway, this latest spate of operations over, I was sent back home again. By now I had had enough. I had had more than enough. No more operations, I wanted to say; I'm ******* sick of them, pick on someone else! To tell the truth, I had just about resigned myself to the fact that I was going to lose the leg by then. In fact, I almost wished that the doctors would decide to chop it off. Then I could have a false one put on and that would be that. At least I would be able to kick on with my life again – which was all I wanted to do. I just wanted it all to be over, one way or the other. I hated all the messing about, not knowing what was going to happen. It was affecting me mentally as well as physically. It was terrible.

And then, through the Injured Jockey's Fund, I was referred to a rehabilitation centre in Camden Town. I'm sure my parents were glad to see the back of me; I'd been a miserable git at home. Now I could be a miserable git in Camden Town – out of harm's way, as it were.

In fact, I wasn't. It was there that I finally began to pick myself up again. Not least because I realised that there were people with far worse injuries than mine. There were jockeys in the centre with smashed shoulder blades, who couldn't raise their hands above their waists. There were others with shattered arms, shattered legs. They had the lot in there. Peter Taylor, Head Lad to Freddy Maxwell (and who went on to train at Newmarket), was in there too. I got to know him quite well. We're friends to this day. He had a fractured skull, couldn't see, hear or smell properly. He had lost his sense of balance. There were members of the public there too; recovering from strokes and so on. It was hard to feel quite so sorry for yourself in that sort of environment.

When I got a letter from the centre saying that I'd been accepted there, I was told to check into a nearby hotel when I arrived. I won't name it. I thought it was going to be really plush. It had a grand sounding name anyway. It turned out to be the absolute pits. It was horrible. Even the husband and wife who ran it were miserable old sods.

But if I was disappointed by the accommodation, I certainly wasn't disappointed by the treatment the centre gave me. With severely limited resources the staff there did a fabulous job. They really made you believe in yourself. They worked damned hard. And all of us patients were made to work hard too. We all had our own individual exercise regimes to follow, but in the mornings we all took part in a warm-up session – to pop music. That was funny, that was. What we must have looked like I don't know. It was like a mad house without the bars in the mornings. When we were allowed out into the gardens we were like two year olds let loose in a field. And it was there that some of us started taking liberties. If we were told we could go out for half an hour, that was it. We would be gone all day. We'd go into town. One bloke, I remember – Michael, he was called – was in a wheelchair. It was hell getting him on and off the buses. The rest of us were on crutches, were all plastered up, were walking with sticks. Once, we went to a pub near Piccadilly. Two of us were on crutches then. It was only when we got back to the centre that we realised that we didn't have them anymore! but did we pay for it the next day! We were in agony. Our legs came up like balloons. It was worth it though. We'd had a laugh.

At weekends I'd leave the centre, go home again. At the time of my accident I was engaged to an insurance office receptionist who I had met at the Orchid Ballroom, Purley.

63

Linda, she was called. When I'd gone into Redhill I'd been quite dependent on her and I think that sustained a relationship which, to be honest, wasn't really there. We got engaged. It was a mistake; we didn't really know each other. We soon realised that fact though and on my first weekend back at home from the centre, we split up. Perhaps to help cheer me up, my father bought me an old Jaguar 3.8 automatic. He got it at a knock-down price, through his connections in the motor-trade. It was an old banger really. But it had a bench seat I could slide my leg along. It cheered me up a lot.

And then I was invited to an Injured Jockey's Fund Gala Ball. There, Peter Taylor introduced me to Thelma Wade, a woman who did a lot of work for the fund. Her husband, Tom, was a Harley Street doctor. She asked me what I was going to do once my leg healed. I told her that I didn't know. "Perhaps we can help," she said. "We've got this place in the country. Come and visit. Maybe a change of scenery will do you good." I decided to keep her invitation in mind.

By this time, with my leg in a leg-guard (a sort of calliper), I was already thinking about what I was going to do next anyway. And against doctor's orders I had even gone abroad. More than that, I went and rode work (the leg-guard enabled me to ride without too much discomfort). I worked in Spain, France, Belgium, Holland, Italy, Cyprus, Norway, Spain. I spent a month or two on the Continent flitting from one place to the next, just turning up at stables whenever I found them. Gizza job! When I got back I needed another small operation to rectify the damage that I had done. After that I started looking for a 'proper' job. Racing, I had been told, was out; there was just no way my leg would stand up to riding work over a prolonged period. My exploits on the Continent were to be my last. I wasn't at all happy about that. It meant that whatever I did was going to be second best, wouldn't be what I wanted to do. But there it was. I just had to get on with things, get on with my life. Forget racing, I told myself. Just forget it.

I got a job with Peter Dominic's off-licence in Banstead, driving a van, making deliveries. I was limping, but I was working. That was the important thing. I was working again. I was earning some sort of living. Up until then I'd been signing on and my parents had supported me; letting me keep all of my benefit for myself. Driving the van, I hoped, having to operate the clutch, would help strengthen my leg too. It did. I also got to learn about wines, which I enjoyed. I stayed in that job for a month, which was how long I said I'd do the job for when I first took it – to see how I got on. It got me started.

After that, I was supposed to go back into hospital again for another operation. The plan was to remove some bone from my hip and use it for another graft. In the event I couldn't face it. My leg felt better and I felt as though I had been through more than enough already. "Leave it," I said. "Let's see how it goes." The doctors weren't convinced that it was the right course of action but they let me have my own way.

So off I went to another job. Van driving again; making deliveries for a butcher – Bell's at Tadworth. And that led on to another job. At the back of the butcher's there was an abattoir. Did I want to work there too? The pay was good . . . largely because the work was so horrific. I took it, started doing the two jobs; the deliveries during the day, the abattoir-work during the evenings. The abattoir-work, I have to say, was worse than horrific. It put me off eating meat for a long time. The smell was something you just can't describe. It never seemed to leave you. It seemed impossible to wash off. You'd be out with friends and you'd think you could smell it, imagine that they could smell it too.

I stayed in those two jobs for about another month or

so. At the same time I was also working part-time in a local hotel, as a bus-boy. I was still desperate to get myself back on track as it were. But I knew that I wasn't doing it. I was just treading water (I was up to my elbows in water, in fact), going nowhere. I didn't want to be doing these dead-end jobs; now that I was fit again I wanted something better. I was coming up for my twenty-seventh birthday. I wanted to be heading somewhere, needed to regain a sense of direction. Brian Jago, the Epsom based stable jockey to Bruce Hobbs, was a good friend by then. He too had been in the Camden Rehabilitation Centre (before my stint there, I should point out), having broken a leg twice within an eighteen month period. One of those breaks, of course, was sustained in the same Sandown pile-up which left Paul so badly injured. Anyway, he offered me a job as his chauffeur, driving him to races. I thought about taking him up on it. It would do me for a while, I thought. But then I got another offer. Again, it wasn't really a job that was going to lead me anywhere . . . but it was definitely something better.

It was a once in a lifetime opportunity.

A SHORT CAREER IN SHOWBIZ

There was a pub at Coldharbour called The Plough. All of Mr. Kerr's owners used to drink there. It was the local watering-hole. All the staff from Crocker's Farm used to go there. In fact, everyone connected with the yard went there; owners, lads, the lot. Once I had the Jag I used to go there to meet up with everyone, have a chat and a gossip. The landlord, Eric Dunning, also worked for Kirby Wires, a company which specialised in special effects for film and television. He had heard about my accident, about all of the problems I was having and one day, out of the blue, he phoned me. "I hear things aren't too good," he said. "But if you're interested, how about coming to work for me? I need an assistant." That was it. That was the start of my short career in showbiz. A week later I found myself at the BBC studios in Shepherd's Bush, working for Eric on a television series set in space. Some years earlier Eric had worked on the film *2001: A Space Odyssey* and the BBC wanted him to do some similar work for them, setting up some of their special effects. It was an incredible experience. The studio we were working in was vast but often it might only be one small part of it that was being used to recreate the whole of outer space. There were black drapes everywhere, mock-up spaceships, huge lights. It was Eric's job to rig some of the actors up on wires so that by using counterweights, pulleys and other bits and pieces we could slowly pull them into shot and make it look as though they were walking in space, weightless. I worked on a gantry above the set where there were these huge metal wheels and all this wire tracing, helped him set it all up. It was great fun. It was quite demanding though too and I had to make sure that I carried out Eric's instructions very carefully. The wire we used was piano wire. If it kinks, it snaps, but apparently it's one of the strongest straight-lift wires you can get. So we just had to make sure that there were no kinks – otherwise our spacemen were going to find out that they were still subject to gravity after all.

After the space series I worked on *Dad's Army*, doing another suspension job; making it look as though Clive Dunn, Mr. Jones, was being hung over the parapet of a bridge, everyone holding his feet, while he tried to grab this secret weapon or something that was coming trundling down the road towards them. That was good fun too. I enjoyed being part of the behind-the-scenes operation, as it were, contributing in my own small way to such a successful comedy series.

And then I went out to Cyprus to work on a film that the Goons were making. *Goons in the Midday Sun* it was called. It was being shot in Kyrenia harbour. Eric had been working on it for a while and, in fact, it was from Kyrenia that he phoned me, asking me to fly out there. The job – another suspension job: hanging people over a castle wall in the harbour – had proved bigger than he thought and he needed some extra machinery brought out, so I brought it with me. It was fabulous going out there. It was so unexpected. The weather was good, everything.

One day though everything went very wrong. This castle wall was some 100ft high. The idea was that we would form a human chain from top to bottom. Someone goes over the wall, hangs on to the top. Someone then climbs over, hangs onto their feet. Someone else then goes and hangs onto their feet. Eventually the last person over finds that his feet are actually on the ground. Anyway, we

Hello Susie Green at Epsom

Tim Thomson Jones wins an amateur race on the grass at Lingfield riding Pinctada for Terry Ramsden

After Pinctada's victory, Terry's racing manager Mick Miller, Tim and myself

Near Down, 1986. I see Terry off

didn't quite allow for the weight of the last person. We were holding them physically. The rope slipped. Eric wouldn't let go though. His hand was really badly cut, really badly burned. The safety rope gave out so quickly that it actually burned into the wood of the telegraph pole or whatever it was that it was tied to. Terrible. Fortunately the stunt men involved escaped with only minor injuries.

I met Spike Milligan, Peter Sellers. But I have to say they weren't very good to work with actually. They were bad news. They kept going back to their hotel when it suited them, being late. It messed everyone around. It didn't help Eric and I, certainly. We'd set everything up and then find that there was no sign of them. In the end the film overran its budget and never got made. But that wasn't only because the production kept getting held up; the main reason was that war broke out. It was then that Turkey invaded Cyprus, claiming that the island was theirs and didn't belong to Greece. We all had to leave – and in a real hurry too. It was chaos. Thousands of pounds worth of equipment got left behind. It just had to be written off. Just like the film itself. Gone. Forget it.

Back home again, Eric soon had another job for me: again working at the BBC studios in Shepherd's Bush. This time we were arranging some special effects for *The Morecambe & Wise Show*. What we did there was stage one of Eric's gags for him. Ernie's out on stage and Eric pokes his head through the gap in the curtain. The next thing you know it's going up and up and up, right the way to the top. He was lying on a platform we'd set up behind the curtain, of course. We could move up or down with more pulleys and wires and so on. It looked good. And all the time he's doing this, Eric is carrying on talking to Ernie. Whey-hey! Ern! Brilliant. And he was a funny man, Eric Morecambe – even when he wasn't trying to be. He was just naturally funny. I liked him.

Working at Shepherd's Bush also meant that I could

visit some of the other studios when we weren't busy. I loved that. I went and saw *Top of the Pops* being made one day. I used to watch it at home all the time, but to actually be there, not as part of the audience, but as someone working for the BBC – brilliant. Pan's People were still dancing on the show then and I got talking to some of them. That was even more exciting. That was really good. It turned out that one of them, Christine, came from Saunderstead, of all places, still lived there. She was a junior dancer with Pan's People. She didn't get to dance on TV every time, but she was part of the team, as it were. And there she was, virtually one of my parents' neighbours. Her parents ran a bakery in Saunderstead and she often worked there at weekends. I made a date with her. In the end we struck up quite a good relationship and after we had been going out together for a few months we got engaged. Before that though, I was off on yet another job. This time working on *The David Nixon Show*. Eric and I helped set up some of his tricks – some of which Paul Daniels now performs. I know how he does them! It was good fun working on that show too. I also enjoyed watching the people who did the warm-ups for the audience before the show started. Some of them were really funny and I think I'm right in saying that one or two of them went on to be in a programme called *The Comedians*. When I do after-dinner speeches now I often think of them.

I must have worked with Eric for about a year, on and off.

LIVING IT UP

With a break in the work for Eric Dunning, I was again left wondering what to do with myself. And it was then that I remembered meeting Thelma Wade at the Injured Jockeys Fund Gala Ball, remembered her invitation to spend a weekend with her and her husband at their home in the country. I decided to take her up on it. So off I went to Sutton Courtenay, near Abingdon in Oxfordshire. They had a lavish estate there, Prior's Court. It was fabulous. When I arrived I was amazed. They had a Bentley convertible (a Corniche) parked outside, a couple of sports cars too. They had beautiful gardens, a swimming pool. It was a fantastic place. Anyway, I stayed there for the weekend. When I was due to go back home again Mrs. Wade asked me why I didn't stay on, work for them.

"What can I do here?" I asked her.

"Mow the lawn," she said. "Keep the house up . . . wash up."

"Where will I live?"

"The annexe."

She persuaded me. I moved into the annexe (basically an extension over the garage), started work. I worked as a chauffeur, gardener, all sorts. I cleaned the swimming pool, did odd-jobs around the house, swept the drive. If it needed doing, I did it. Looking back on it now it seems crazy. Unreal. I wasn't paid for any of it; I just lived at Prior's Court for free, ate my meals with the family. Occasionally, though, the Wade's would have guests over and I'd act as a sort of butler for them. I'd even dress the part. Mrs. Wade would ring this little bell and I'd appear. You rang? I have to say, I didn't enjoy it much – not only playing the butler, but the whole manservant bit. It wasn't me. Rightly or wrongly I did feel like I was being used. I felt like I was a gimmick or something, that was it.

But if I did occasionally feel resentful about my role at Prior's Court, I soon got over it. There were numerous compensations. To begin with, I got to know a lot of people from the horse-racing world who the Wades were friendly with and who would often visit the house. Ken Payne was one of them. 'Window' Payne we used to call him because he had been a window cleaner before he started training horses. He was Mr. Selling Races. He picked those off left, right and centre. He was a cracking trainer. His jockey (who was then champion apprentice) was Johnny Curant and Johnny would often visit the house too.

Now what I haven't yet mentioned is the fact that the Wades only used Prior's Court at weekends; the rest of the time they were in London, staying at their home there, in Harley Street. That meant that for the rest of the week I had the run of the place. And I made the most of it. Jesus, I really lived it up. For example, Johnny and I would take the Corniche, drive into Abingdon. Christine was working in Barcelona then. She had been appearing in a panto-mime at Streatham when some auditions had come up for a programme on Spanish television. She had passed. Off she went. I had got into the habit of sending flowers to her. Eileen, who is now my wife, used to work at the florist's where I used to send them from. It was a laugh. Johnny and I would turn up in the Corniche. He'd sit outside in it while I went into the shop. He'd press the button which made the top go up and down. Up and down it would go. Up and down. He never tired of it. I fancied Eileen by now and was asking her out. I told her that the car was mine, that I owned a place in the country. She thought that I was a flash git – a flash git who was already engaged to someone – and said no. In fact, when she saw me coming, I later discovered, she would try and duck out the back of the shop to avoid me. If she saw me in the square she'd shoot off in the opposite direction. I'd chase off after her and she'd start walking faster and faster until she was practically running. Hilarious.

It was coming up to Christmas by this time and I hadn't seen Christine for a while. I decided to go and visit her. I phoned her, arranged things. I collected some presents that her family wanted me to deliver to her, set off. My plan was to drive down there, spend Christmas Eve with her, drive back again on Christmas Day. I could then spend Boxing Day with my family. I had sold the Jag by then, bought an orange MGB. I was Jack-the-Lad. I was looking forward to the drive. I thought it would be quite an adventure.

And it was. To begin with the ferry crossing from Southampton to Bilbao was terrible. There was a huge storm in the Bay of Biscay and we were thrown about all over the shop. I couldn't sleep. Not only because we were rolling about so much, but because of the noise of all the chains attached to the cars in the hold rattling. It was horrendous. I thought that by the time we docked my car would probably be bashed to bits, and I thought I was going to be very sick. Eventually though we arrived at Bilbao. I'm okay, the car's okay. I set off for Barcelona – on my own, a map in my lap, speaking no Spanish whatsoever. It was a beautiful drive. I made one stop, one detour – to look at a bullring. Finally I reached Barcelona. Bad news. No Christine. She's gone to Madrid. The show she was in was doing a one-off there or something. So straight away I'm back on the road again. Crazy. I drove all night. When I got to Madrid I was knackered. I go to the flat where Christine's staying and what do I find? She's there all right – but she's in bed with some Jose, Pedro or Miguel. I was devastated, gutted. I slung the stuff I'd brought for her through the door, got back in the car again. I couldn't believe it; it seemed like I was destined to do nothing but drive. I drove from Madrid all the way to Calais. It was sheer bloody madness. I was falling asleep at the wheel. Shortly after leaving Madrid I ran out of petrol. It was still late at night. I pulled in at this filling station, found I had no money. What did I do? I filled up, drove off down the road like stink. That's what I did. It kept me awake though. For hours afterwards I thought that every car that came up behind me was someone from the station chasing me. And when I passed a cop car! I was sure that they would be on the look out for me. There's the bastard! After him! Worrying about being caught kept me going, kept my foot down. Somehow I managed to stick to my original timetable, stupid though it was; I was back home again for Boxing Day. Christine and I are still in touch, as it happens. She's married, has two kids, lives in Rome where her husband runs a couple of restaurants and she runs a dancing school. We still have a laugh about that trip of mine over to Spain to see her.

So by the time I got back to Prior's Court my life had suddenly changed. I was ready for a fresh start. And I started renewing my efforts to get Eileen to come out with me. I told her that things between me and Christine were over and eventually she gave in. I took her back to Prior's Court for tea. Soon we were going out together. And I discovered that she knew Prior's Court quite well, had nicked apples from the orchard there when she was a kid. She knew who owned it all along.

Meanwhile, I'm still odd-jobbing at the house. I'm still having a laugh there too. There was an outbuilding in the grounds nicknamed the ICU – the Intensive Care Unit. It was an open, thatched barn. Inside it there was a juke-box, table-football, a tennis-table. It was a playroom really. Quite often I'd invite other jockey-friends around: Trevor Rogers, Dennis McKay, Dave Atkinson. We'd stay in there for hours. It was good fun. And then in the evenings we'd often go to a nightclub, The Riverside, just outside Abingdon.

But it wasn't long before I began to feel that playing Jack-of-all-Trades half the week, Jack-the-Lad the rest just wasn't good enough. It wasn't getting me anywhere. It was time to knuckle down again, do something to get on in life. Now it so happened that there were some disused stables at the back of the house. I began to wonder if I could do something with them. I asked the Wades if they would mind me having a go. They didn't. Tom Wade even suggested that we get our own horses in. And that's just what we did. We got to work. We cleaned up the stables, called them Prior's Court Stables, bought in half a dozen horses. Mrs. Wade had some horses with Clive Brittain then and he gave me some advice about things. So too did Ken Payne. I started off by running a small livery business at Prior's Court and for about a year I had between eight and ten horses there. Clive Brittain and Ken Payne maintained their interest by sending me horses to break in for them. Mrs. Wade had a couple of horses who weren't really progressing with Ken so I got those too. Things were good. I had even been given planning permission to build a second six-box yard if I needed to. It could have been twelve but that would have meant closing some of the horses off and not giving them open views. I didn't want that. I think you have to allow a horse some sort of view of things just to keep it from getting bored. It's only fair. During that year the only other full-time member of staff I had with me was my brother Brian. We had to keep running costs to a minimum. Having said that though, I had no shortage of jockeys to ride work for me. Johnny Curant rode out for me, of course, but I also had Dave Atkinson, Dennis McKay and Trevor Rogers who would come over whenever I asked them to. And my brother, Paul, then apprenticed at Epsom, would come over occasionally too. Sometimes it seemed as though I had more jockeys than horses.

The best horse in the yard was probably African Winner, but none of them were really that good. None of them were world beaters. Not by a long chalk. But one of them, Royal Cadet, had already made a name for himself by the time he came to me, early in 1976, towards the end of my time at Prior's Court. He was the first horse in the country to have been ridden by a professional female jockey. Jane McDonald rode him in an apprentices' race at Doncaster the previous March. March 20th 1975, to be exact. They finished eleventh.

But back to the summer of '74. When I was starting up the livery business, I went to a saddler's at East Ilsley to buy some head-collars and other bits and pieces that I needed. I couldn't park on the road so I took the car round the back. There was a car under a tarpaulin there. When I left the shop I couldn't resist having a look. And what did I find? It was an old E-type Jaguar, full of chickens. Anyway, I thought nothing of it at the time; drove back to Prior's Court with all the tack I'd bought. But that night it started bugging me. Bug, bug, bug., First thing in the morning I phoned the bloke at the shop, told him that I'd noticed the E-type he had at the back of the house, asked if it was for sale. It turned out that it had been his son's, that his son had died and he just hadn't got around to getting rid of it. In the end I bought it. £500. I went over there with a friend, towed it back to Prior's Court on a trailer. It was in a right state. But what a car! It was a convertible, had wire-wheels, Le Mans headlights. It was a bit special, even for an E-type. We tried to start it up there and then . . . and it almost turned over. I couldn't believe it. After that it became a labour of love for me. I'd ride out the horses in the morning, work on the car during the day. Eventually I sent it off to a local garage. The engine came out, the exhaust (what there was left of it; most of it had just rotted away), the wheels, the lot. The wheels were sent away to be re-chromed. The body, which I had already stripped down, was resprayed, the underside sealed. Soon it's back to its original colour: white. Out come the seats, remade. Out comes the dashboard, remade. Off comes the hood, remade. In the end this car looks like a million dollars. It almost cost me that much to get it to that state too. Fortunately though, I didn't have to stump up for it in one whack. It was £400, say, for this, £200 for that, £400 for the other. I think it all came to about £2000 in the end. And I got a mint-condition E-type out of it. A bargain!

But while I succeeded in transforming the E-type, I didn't succeed in transforming Prior's Court. The big drawback was the lack of facilities. I didn't really have any. Running a livery yard was one thing, but training horses to actually run was quite another. I would have loved to have trained horses for the Wades . . . but it just wasn't feasible. Not at Prior's Court. It had been a pipe-dream thinking that we could.

I'd reached the end of the road, as it were, at Prior's Court. After two years, then, I left. Eileen and I were thinking of getting married so I needed to get on – and at Prior's Court that just wasn't happening for me. I moved back in with my parents, who were then living in Bookham, began to think about getting another job in horseracing.

And it was then that Nobber Darnell came back into my life. He had left Godalming and was now working as a stud groom at a place called Wheatlands Manor in Finchampstead near Camberley in Surrey. It was owned by an Italian family, the Zandonas. He phoned me up and said look, it's not happening now, but I think that they want someone to train horses for them. Well, that was just the sort of thing that I was looking for. I went out there to have a look at things. I then spoke to Mr. Zandona on the phone and he confirmed that if things progressed well on

81

the breeding side, yes, he wanted to have his own horses trained at Wheatlands Manor under a private trainer. He said he would be interested in me filling that role.

In the meantime, I'm still looking for a job. The word's going around. And that's what does the trick for me. The trainer Merrick Francis, who had taken over Crocker's Farm from Alec Kerr, called me, said his Head Lad was leaving in October, was I interested? I told him I was, but also told him about the situation with regard to the Zandonas. If the job of private trainer came up at Wheatlands Manor, I said, I would have to leave him. He understood, accepted that. "I just need a Head Lad now," he said. "I'm desperate and you'd be perfect for me." So that was it. It was decided. Come October, I would take over as Head Lad for him.

Which still left me with a few months to spare. What I did then was go and work with my brother-in-law, Mick (he and Mary had married by now), working as a plasterer. But the main event which took place at that time was that Eileen and I got married. The 18th September 1976, at Culham, just outside Abingdon. We had Nicky Adams, who was then apprenticed to Mr. Johnson-Houghton but who had occasionally worked at Prior's Court, as our best-man; none of my brothers wanted to do it. He was fifteen, had to stand on a chair. I was thirty-two, Eileen was ten years younger. Eileen was waitressing in a Berni Inn then, still living at home with her parents in Steventon. The plan was that we would move to Chertsey. Eileen's cousin and her husband owned a house there and wanted to rent out a flat on the top floor. It was all set up. In fact, everything seemed nicely set up. I was driving around in an E-type, had some money saved up, had two job offers. I had a plastering job to keep me ticking over, Eileen and I were planning our wedding, planning what we were going to do with our future. It was a really good time in my life. I felt so good that, in fact, like a plonker I even went back to playing football again. The leg felt okay. I chanced it. Luck seemed to be on my side. Sod it, I thought. Go for it.

A couple of nights before my Stag Night proper, I went out in the E-type having been invited to a nightclub in Crawley where all the air-hostesses from Gatwick went. I had a cracking time there, a right good night out. At four in the morning, driving this girl home to her flat, I got stopped by the police. Well, I forgot all about it afterwards, didn't I? Eileen and I got married. A few months later I got a summons through the post with this ridiculous statement on it. I had to hide it. Eileen played like she didn't know anything about it, but occasionally kept bringing the subject up. She was just doing it to get back at me, of course. Eventually she told me. "I know all about that night in Crawley," she said. "You can stop trying to pretend now." It was a laugh.

Shortly before that I'd sold the E-type anyway. I got £4,500 for it. We spent the money on furniture and so on for the flat.

But we weren't at the flat for long, of course. The job at Coldharbour with Merrick Francis meant that we had to find another flat – in Dorking. That job eventually came up in January. I was going to start the new year married, in a new job and with the possibility of becoming a private trainer on the horizon.

Not bad, I thought.

HEAD LAD

The flat Eileen and I finally found once my move back to Coldharbour was confirmed was at a place called Ainsty Grange. We moved in there just before Christmas. It was a beautiful old house surrounded by rhododendrons and huge lawns. The rooms were enormous. We used to joke about getting a lodger in. And so high too. In all there were thirty-two people living there and basically that's what made it a rather unpleasant place to live in in the end. Although you had your own flat, you never really felt as though you had your privacy. There were just so many people around. It was more like a hotel.

On the plus side it was handy for work. I only had to nip over the back fence and walk half a mile to the yard. I would stop and talk to the cows, the pigs and the chickens at Ainsty Grange Farm. It would only take me seven minutes or so to get there. Eileen, who had got a job at a florist's in Leatherhead, had the rough end of the stick. She had to walk all the way down the driveway to catch the bus to work. The driveway was as long as a road. It took longer to get from the main road to the house than it took for me to go over the fence at the back of the house and get to work.

Merrick Francis (whose father is the novelist and former jockey Dick Francis, of course) had been assistant trainer to quite a few people in his time. He was now keen to get on in his own right. He was ambitious. And he had attracted several good owners too. He had about thirty horses in the yard. His assistant trainer was Patrick Haslam. The first season I was with him I think he had some of the best horses he ever had. Black Sabbath was one I remember. The local butcher had quite a few good horses with us too. We won a lot of good races. In fact, we had twenty-one winners in that first season, I think I'm right in saying.

One of the worst horses we had was called Eric Stanley. It scared the pants off me, that animal. It was always bolting with me – which brought back some pretty unhappy memories, to say the least. It would bolt with everyone who tried to ride him. One day he took off down this road with me. Could I pull him up? It was hopeless. We're full-tilt all the way. I knew I was going to have to bale out if I got the chance. Luckily for me he turned to run around the side of a house at the end of the road. There was a grass verge there. There was also a pond. Off I went, missed the pond, thank God, and Eric Stanley went on his way without me. He was a bastard. I won't forget him in a hurry. He made me tear my jodhpurs too. Bastard.

I wasn't at Merrick's very long, but again I had to earn the respect of the staff under me – just as I had at Crocker's Farm when I had been Travelling Head Lad for Alec Kerr. Again I had to be hard, had to make sure that they didn't take too many liberties with me. In fact, I had to be harder than I had been at Crocker's Farm. The staff were a bit resentful of me when I got the job. Merely because I was new, on the one hand. Because they found me a bit too much of a perfectionist on the other. They didn't want to work quite as hard as I wanted them too. It worried me quite a lot. I let them jibe me a bit to begin with, but I knew that things couldn't go on like that; I was being too soft, couldn't motivate people, couldn't get done the things that needed doing. I told Eileen I didn't know what to do about it. And that was the final straw, as it were. I couldn't just sit on the fence anymore, put up with the silly comments I heard behind my back. I knew then that I just had to sort them out – just do it. And I did. I put into practice everything I had learned from Mardie again. But what I also did was take two of them out into the yard and simply gave them a good hiding. Smack! I let people know that I meant business, that I was going to do my job. And I did. I sorted things out, did my job. They did theirs. In the end we all got on okay. After that initial spat things were never better. I think they began to respect me a bit more then. We all started going to the pub together – The Plough. It was just a phase we all had to go through. We just had to get to know one another. It all worked out fine in the end. It was only really at all difficult for about a month or so.

All in all Eileen and I had a good time at Ainsty Grange. It was the first place we had had together. I got back into the swing of working with stable staff, with horses again. Eileen enjoyed working at the shop in Leatherhead. It was interesting for me to be back in Coldharbour again where I knew so many people, being able to call in at The Plough again on a regular basis, see Eric. We were happy there.

No sooner had I got into the swing of things though than it began to look as though the Zandonas were about to take the plunge into having some of their horses trained at Wheatland's Manor – just as they had planned. I went over to Finchampstead to see them. There was Arthur Zandona, his wife, Celia, their son, George and their daughter, Cecilia. They were a wealthy family. Celia Zandona's father had come over from Italy and had set up Valley Coaches. She and Arthur were involved in property management and had numerous other business interests too. Anyway, they were keen to kick on with their plans to have their horses trained there, so they made me an offer. What they said was that they couldn't set me up straight away but what they could do was offer me a bungalow (which was pretty basic; more like a shed) in the grounds while they negotiated the purchase of a place called Shepperland's Copse opposite the estate. It was a chicken farm. The house there was beautiful. It wasn't lavish. It was just a nice little three-bedroomed house set in its own grounds. Ideal. The plan was for Eileen and I to move in there, then they'd gut the rest of the place, lay down an all-weather gallop, build the boxes, a barn – the lot. That's where I'd train. In the meantime, they said, stay in the bungalow, work with Nobber (Nobber Darnell) getting the young horses prepared and so on.

It sounded good to me – and I wanted to be involved in things from the off, right from the start. So I said yes to their offer; I'd do it.

From Head Lad to private trainer in a few months.

Things were definitely looking up.

THE ITALIAN CONNECTION

They were fantastic people, the Zandonas; enthusiastic, generous . . . as supportive as they come. Celia Zandona didn't really know that much about horses. She once saw a horse with its fifth leg hanging out, thought it had injured itself. But she made up for it with her enthusiasm. She got really involved emotionally. In business, she was obviously quite hard – as, of course, you have to be to be successful. The language she could use on occasions. Once, I was in the stewards' room with her when an enquiry was announced. "What the ******* hell do they mean, stewards' enquiry?" she yelled. And when she couldn't find Arthur on the course she'd let rip then too. Arth-ur! He'd come running. I liked her a lot.

Arthur was just the opposite of Celia; as quiet as she was loud. And he did know his horses. He was always in the yard, always keen to know how the horses were getting on, wanting to know which races they had been entered for and so on. He took a really lively interest, couldn't have been more determined that the whole enterprise would succeed. I loved having him around.

Eileen and I weren't in the 'shed' for very long. True to their word the Zandonas bought Shepperland's Copse, did the house up for us, started on the training facilities. I was granted a permit by the Jockey Club to set up as a private trainer – training flat horses for the family. We were away. But not before the Zandonas had stumped up for Eileen and I to go on holiday to Barbados. I said they were generous.

We had twelve boxes in the yard when I started training. The Zandonas started me off with nine horses. George Zandona who was their bloodstock manager, owned most of those. My first runner was a slag of a horse, a horrible little mare called El Regalo. It belonged to Celia Zandona and she had previously had it in training with, I think, John Benstead. It was no good. Nor were a few of the other horses. I had to tell them: "Look, this lot are no good. We've got to buy some new ones." And that's what we did. They bought in some two year-olds. It was also the only time in my life when I've had two year-olds bought for me from Kentucky – from the Keenland Sales. They bought two horses from there: Dollar Pocket and Hello Susie Greene. The Zandona's named most of the other horses they bought in after various songs. Hello Susie Greene. Pennies From Heaven. Sunnybanks Angel.

The first year or so was pretty quiet really. It was inevitable. Things had to have time to settle down. But that was on the stable front. On the home front things were bloody noisy. Eileen and I had our first child then: a son, Robin. His teething troubles kept me awake many a night . . . and eventually landed me in front of the stewards and the Jockey Club.

Dollar Pocket, one of the horses which came from Kentucky, was the first horse I ever got fined over. What a farce that was. It had trouble with its balls, Dollar Pocket, sometimes used to hurt itself when it was galloping. Eileen came up with a brilliant suggestion: put some of Robin's teething gel on them. And that's what I did. Trouble was, the gel contained a proscribed substance, Lignocaine. After the race Dollar Pocket failed a routine dope test. Not because this stuff had got into its blood or urine; it had just run down into the sample in the horse's sweat. Anyway, I'm off to Portman Square, aren't I? £350 fine under rule 53 relating to prohibited substances. The minimum fine but even so. I thought that was really off.

89

Eileen had come up with the bloody idea – she should have copped it, not me.

When I look back at my time with the Zandonas, I remember just how hard I had to work at Wheatland's Manor. Basically, I was a one-man band there. Early morning feeds, mucking-out, tacking up: I did it. Boxing the horses up to ride them work: me again. And once I got there it would be the same routine. Get one out, ride it, put it back. Four horses. Hard work. It was exhausting. And to do that every day, day in, day out. Hard work.

Occasionally David Atkinson would come over and help me ride work. That helped. His career was on the slide then and he was looking for a bit of a break, just as he had when he had ridden for me at Prior's Court. We helped one another, in fact. He might not have been a first class jockey, but then I wasn't a first class trainer. We made a good team. He rode work on the horses (he was especially good with the more difficult rides that I couldn't handle properly) and when I had to go away for some reason or other he would cover in the yard for me. I put him up for quite a few rides.

And it was David who rode my first winner. Lady Tartown. We took her to Warwick for a little race, the Man Appeal Maiden Fillies' Stakes (Div. II) on 9th June 1979 where she was the outsider of the field. The favourite for the race, Sarigue, was odds-on. Sarigue was trained by Peter Walwyn, who was *the* trainer then. Pat Eddery was riding. Lady Tartown had a lot in common with a little horse I have now, Walk In The Park. Short, stubby-boned, with a huge back end and virtually nothing up front – a drag-racer type of horse; all the power behind the saddle. She had run a good race on her previous outing at Newbury, where she had led a good field until the final furlong, and although she still wasn't fully wound up I was hopeful of another good run. Having led from the start, we came into the final furlong out in front, Pat Eddery and

Sarigue breathing down our neck. Celia Zandona was going crazy (and shouting her head off). I was standing up in the stands with her. I didn't think we were going to make it, but we did. We got home by a head. I was absolutely ecstatic. It was fantastic seeing Mrs. Zandona's colours flash by the post in first place. Fantastic. I'll never forget that moment. And the press interest we then got! They didn't mention my clothes to begin with; to begin with there was nothing really noticeable about them. Since I travelled with the horses and only had a groom, Sarah, to help me, I usually wore old clothes, tatty stuff. I'd be washing the horses down, all that. When we got back home I'd be doing evening stables, no matter what time of night I got back. It had to be done. I had to do it. Looking snappy wasn't a consideration then. I couldn't afford that luxury. That night I went and got drunk as a skunk at a local pub, The Tally-Ho.

Lady Tartown's win was, of course, a real high. Tremendous. As far as the Zandonas were concerned I could have stayed in bed for the next week; they wouldn't have cared. We had had a winner! But then shortly after that we suffered a couple of reverses. The first wasn't so much a reverse, in fact; it was a devastating blow. A few days later Arthur and I were having a cup of coffee. We were having a laugh and a joke about how well things were going. Suddenly we heard all this banging and crashing outside. We ran straight out into the yard – and there's Lady Tartown on the deck in her box. We got her up again, discovered, of all the things to happen, that she had broken her leg. It was a terrible – terrible – moment. Only minutes before we had been walking around the yard, had been giving her a pat over the stable door. She never ran again. What she'd done was shatter her pastern, dislocate the fetlock joint on her off hind. The vets put a screw in the pastern, reset the dislocation and she went off to stud. Gone. After the high of her win, that was a real kick in the teeth. It brought us all right down again. It was horrible.

It was hard putting Lady Tartown's accident behind us. It's hard putting any accident like that behind you. But we started getting on with things again. Only to then suddenly have the stable struck down with a virus. It was bad. Just when we wanted to capitalise on the attention we had got, we had nothing. We couldn't run anything – or if we did they were just getting beaten. We ran Hello Susie Greene at Chepstow, for example. She never got into the race at all, trailed in last of the four runners. On the form of her previous run, when she was beaten half a length by Pat Eddery on Miss Quaver at Kempton, she should have been in with a good chance. The Zandona's, who were devout Catholics, came up with an idea: get a priest in, get the horses blessed. And that's what they did. It was brilliant. This priest came round to the yard, sprinkled the lot of them – and me – with holy water, said a few words, the lot. The horses continued to cough for quite a while afterwards, but the virus eventually lifted and we got going again. Whether having the horses blessed helped I don't know. But what did help was being allowed to use some gallops at Billingbear Park (where Con Horgan now trains) originally used by Norah Wilmot. Working the horses on those really helped me to assess just how well the horses had recovered, just how much they were coming on.

Now the pendulum swings the other way. Now we're on the up again. We add to Lady Tartown's win, start picking up a few little races. Things take off for us. Hello Susie Greene wins at Chester. Pennies From Heaven hacks up by five lengths in the Belmead Selling Handicap at Windsor after leading from the off. Petite Realm wins at Chester. Sunnybanks Angel wins at Brighton and then at Salisbury. We even enter a horse in the Derby. That was a laugh. The horse was called Waverley Hall. It was named after Zandona's office in London. I backed it to finish last, thinking that it definitely would be. Instead of backing it at 500–1 to win, 250–1 to be placed, I took 2–1 for him to be last. The bastard went and beat one. I couldn't believe it. More realistically, we also took Hello Susie Greene to France, to run in the Prix Robert Papin. She had a good chance there, no doubt about it. I knew it was worth going for. Win that and we'd certainly make our mark. So off we went. In the event we never even ran. The ground had been hard. The course had been watered – which is something the French do rather more readily than we do over here. And then it had rained. In fact, there had been a deluge. Suddenly the going was all wrong. It was really holding. The French classified it as good but it was soft. What is regarded in France as being good ground is re-garded by us as being soft. It wasn't what Hello Susie Greene wanted at all. To be honest though, I don't think she would have won anyway. Once we got there I realised that she had boiled over. She had gone over the top. Basically I was a week late for the race. So it goes.

By now, to return to the subject of my sartorial habits once more, I was wearing some pretty eye-catching clothes. As I've already said, I wore them partly to get some attention. I was a new trainer on the scene – a small trainer – I wanted to make a bit of a splash, get myself noticed. Not to attract new owners; as a private trainer I wasn't in a position to take them on. At that time I did it simply to stir things up a bit, to add a bit of showbiz, a bit of razzmatazz . . . a bit of colour. Why not? Racing was, and still is, too conservative, too full of snobbery and stuffiness. I started turning up wearing all sorts of golfing gear. But bright golfing gear. The brightest I could find. The Press loved it. Plenty of people didn't, sure, but then I didn't think much of what they would come to the races wearing. You couldn't tell them apart. I just want to free things up a bit. I didn't want to have to wear a uniform.

Talking of which . . .

There was an army base near Finchampstead. It was not funny; the guards at the gate often didn't have guns with them, they had sticks. Anyway, one morning this army helicopter came over the yard. I couldn't believe it. I was having my breakfast at the time, could hear it getting closer and closer . . . until eventually it was right overhead. Well you can imagine, the horses were going crazy. The wooden boxes that they were in weren't that strong and they were kicking them down. I ran outside, started shouting up at this thing. Piss off! Stupid bastards! Look what you're doing! Piss off! It was terrible. The whole place was shaking. Off this helicopter went. I went and had a look at the horses. They've all got cuts, grazes. And then this helicopter comes back again. Now I'm throwing stones at it. I was desperate. Ray Chiarella, a Canadian friend who had been having breakfast with me, was out there with me. We both jumped in the car, drove straight over to the gatehouse. What have the guards got today? Machine-guns. They wouldn't let us in. Round to the other gate. Same story. Still ranting and raving like a lunatic, I demanded to see someone. That bastard helicopter caused havoc in my yard, I told them. They weren't interested. "I'm going to see someone then," I told them.

"You're not going in."

"I am going in."

And in I went. The next thing we knew, we were brought to a halt by a jeep pulling up in front of us, broadside on. Out jumped this Sergeant with some more guards. Again I started ranting and raving. The Sergeant went off to get someone to speak to me about what the helicopter had been doing. Meanwhile, the guards kept us standing there at gunpoint. It was crazy.

Anyway, the Sergeant finally returns. He's got an officer with him. A Captain somebody or other. "Where's your ship?" I asked him. It turned out that H.R.H. Prince

94

Philip was visiting the base. The Captain told me that they had thought there might be an IRA sniper in a field near my yard. They'd sent the helicopter to flatten the grass, flush the sniper out.

"We have to act on every tip we get," he said.

"If I did that," I said. "I'd be skint."

A few days later I got a visit from some big brass from the base. They turned up in the yard in a limo with a flag on the bonnet (hello, I thought, Prince Philip's come to visit me now), apologised for the trouble they had caused me and that was it. We were pals from then on. They didn't disturb me, I didn't disturb them.

The good press I got during my time at Shepperland's Copse eventually led to a number of owners contacting me, wanting me to train their horses for them. Of course, I couldn't; I was a private trainer, not a public trainer. But then the Zandonas, seeing what was happening, suggested that I should go public. More than that; they said they would help me.

Before moving to Finchampstead, the Zandonas had lived in Epsom. They had connections there. In fact, they had had horses in training there in the past. And it was through their connections with Epsom that they learned that Scobie Breasley was about to give up his yard at South Hatch, Epsom (where Reg Akehurst now trains). Scobie was retiring as a trainer to become racing manager to Ravi Tikkoo. A company, South Hatch Racing Stables Ltd. was set up between myself, Ray Chiarella (who wanted to get more involved in horses than he had previously been) and another businessman, Jim McCaughey, a friend of Ray's who already had several horses in training with Michael Stoute. South Hatch Racing, it was agreed, would rent the yard from Scobie. The Zandonas confirmed that they wanted to keep their horses in training with me there.

It was decided that I would take over at South Hatch at the beginning of the New Year. 1981.

In my two seasons training for the Zandonas I had sent out twelve winners. Nine in that tremendously successful first year (from thirty runs and kicked off, of course, by Lady Tartown's win) three in 1980.

Now, I only had to build on that success.

THE REAL THING

South Hatch was a really old yard. Some of the boxes were brick-built and even had gas-lamps in them. Walter Nightingall had owned it before Scobie Breasley took over there. It had quite a history, a tradition. Walter Nightingall had trained the 1943 Derby winner, Straight Deal, there. He had also sent out the 1965 2,000 Guineas winner, Niksar, from South Hatch. I felt really excited about moving in, being a part of all that. I suddenly felt that I had arrived. I knew that I hadn't cracked it, not by a long chalk; I was only just starting off. But I was a proper trainer now. The real thing.

Scobie Breasley was really helpful when I took over from him at South Hatch. He sold me his old tack, his feed-bins and so on, gave me any advice I asked for. Whenever I had a problem he was available. He also persuaded several of his owners to come to me. That was even more helpful. One of those owners was a man called Vasant Advani. He was to come to play a major role in my life when the time eventually came for me to leave South Hatch, as I'll explain later.

In my first year at South Hatch, which had forty-three boxes in all, I had twenty horses. The Zandonas, Ray Chiarella and Jim McCaughey owned most of those, of course, but I also had another big owner who came to me: Noel Suter, who was a businessman based on the Isle of Man. He sent me six horses in one batch. None of the horses were particularly clever, true, but that's a situation which most young trainers have to contend with. You get bad horses, sour horses, horses with problems or with little or no potential. Owners just aren't prepared to entrust really good horses to you – not unless you're very, very lucky or you already have a reputation built up for yourself. You just have to get on with things. You make the most of what you've got. And then, if you can prove yourself, then you might get some good horses. Better horses, anyway.

It was hard, that first year at South Hatch. It was a real struggle. The Zandona horses – Hello Susie Greene, Petite Realm, Waverley Hall and so on – were especially slow to readjust to their new surroundings. A change of yard changes a horse's metabolism. It has to get used to the change of water, scenery, the yard itself. Everything. It all affects them. It takes time. I only had one stable girl, one jockey (Bryn Crossley, who was retained by Jim McCaughey) working for me. That didn't help either. I had a lot – a lot – of work to do. And then, on top of all that, I had to readjust my training methods too, try to settle into a new routine which suited the facilities which I had at South Hatch. At Shepperland's Copse I had had to box horses up to take them out to work. At South Hatch the gallops were practically on the doorstep. Perhaps because of this, I tended to overwork the horses at first. I would give them some road work to toughen up their tendons, work them on the gallops . . . and to begin with I just did too much. Simple as that. I did too much too often. I underestimated just how much work I was actually giving the horses. And, of course, the result was that I sent quite a few of them over the top. They reached peak fitness before I even got them to the racecourse. Stupid. My fault. But, as I say, it was simply a case of trying to settle into some sort of routine again, to find the right balance. That was the problem. It took some time to do.

Swashbuckling won two races that Spring, including the H.S. Persse Memorial Handicap at Kempton, which earned me my first trophy. Before that again, in May 1981 he landed the Whitstable Handicap at Folkestone, ridden by Bryn Crossley. I had my first double that day. Petite Realm, ridden by Joe Mercer, took the Metropole Challenge Cup on the same card. He was a huge horse, Swashbuckling, had to have a double-size box. He also needed soft ground to show his form. When he jarred himself up in the Northumberland Plate we had to put him away. He had bad legs, it wasn't worth taking the risk with him.

My very first winner as a public trainer should have been ridden by Lester Piggott. He was due to ride Petite Realm for me at Sandown. But then he had that horrific accident at Epsom, nearly having his ear torn off in the stalls. South Hatch is right next to Epsom racecourse and Eileen heard the noise of the crowd. Joe Mercer came in for the ride instead. The previous day several of my stable staff had gone down with food poisoning so that morning I had had to ride out five consecutive lots all on my own. When I got to Sandown I was knackered. After that winner though I forgot how tired I was. It was fantastic. Joe and I are still close friends now. We play golf together. I keep meaning to show him a picture of him riding Petite Realm because I'm sure he's forgotten that he won that race for me.

But although the horses were running well enough by now, Eileen and I still hadn't settled in Epsom. We still didn't feel at home there. We didn't like the house much. There was too much traffic (having a horse run loose at Epsom is a big worry). People weren't very friendly towards us. Mick Haynes was welcoming (and we're still friends now, enjoy meeting up at the races), but a lot of the other trainers there weren't. There was a sort of dog-eat-dog atmosphere at Epsom. I get on better with any number of Epsom trainers now than I ever did when I was there.

And things got worse. We sent Hello Susie Greene for a race at Epsom. She was in her box when the sprinkler system suddenly came on. She spooked, slipped up and fractured her pelvis. She had to be put down. I had to phone the Zandonas with the news. Like me, they were devastated. Hello Susie Greene had been our pride and joy. Having lost Lady Tartown already it was just diabolical luck. I think that it was then that the Zandonas began to question whether they really wanted to continue in racing. I think that that was definitely a turning point for them. Anyway, not long after that they decided to get out. Not only because of losing Hello Susie Greene really, but also because their bloodstock interests were taking up so much of their time, because that side of things was demanding more and more of their attention. But our association had been a success.

With the Zandonas gone, I had to start looking even harder for new owners, new horses. Brian Jago, stable jockey to Bruce Hobbs, was based nearby and he was a great help in that respect. Not only did he come in and ride work for me, he also introduced me to a couple of good owners. Come our second year we had thirty-five horses in the yard. Jim McCaughey had taken over the lease of South Hatch and at last things looked good again.

My best horses have almost always been bought straight out of a field or at the sales after I'd seen them in the field first. All of them have gone on to be good winners. That December I bought Bajan Sunshine out of a field. He was a two year-old then and was a really sorry sight. He looked horrific. He was so weak he could hardly get out of his own way. He had various skin abrasions. He had redworm. But I liked him. He had been recommended to me, he was always trying to jump out of his paddock he was so spirited and he was bred to stay. I bought him for peanuts. When I got him home, he suddenly began to improve. He began to strengthen up, tried to jump out of the paddock even more, began to do some good work on the gallops. And it was then that I began to wonder ... Once I'd become a proper, public trainer, someone had asked me what my ambition was. I'd told them that I wanted to train a Cesarewitch winner. Could Bajan Sunshine be good enough? The more I thought about it, the more I began to think that he could be – if I was. I only had to find out if he really did have the ability. When I told Ray Chiarella that I really did rate the horse, Ray bought him.

On 29th March 1982 Bryn Crossley rode a double for me, on Amarone and Heathen Prince at Folkestone. After that I began to think that Folkestone must be a lucky course for me; the previous May, of course, I'd had a double there with Swashbuckling and Petite Realm.

On 21st April 1982, African Pearl, a horse that had come to me from Gavin Pritchard-Gordon's yard – and which had already picked up the Westenhanger House Handicap at Folkestone – won the City and Suburban at Epsom, again ridden by Bryn Crossley. In those days the City and Suburban was one of the most important races on the calendar; up there with the best of them. It was my biggest win to date.

I then sent Bajan Sunshine out for the first time. I ran him in a small stakes race at Folkestone. The trip was too short for him – one and a quarter miles – but he ran well, finished third. Johnny Curant rode him for me, was very impressed with him too. It was a good start.

As I've already said, my stable jockey at South Hatch was Bryn Crossley who was retained by Jim McCaughey. He was a good jockey and I never had any complaints about his riding. He rode some good winners for me. No problem. Unfortunately, our relationship came to an end at the close of the 1982 season when, for tax reasons, Jim McCaughey decided to take his horses to Ireland for a year, having them in training with Con Collins, John Oxx and Michael Kauntz – who just to show how interconnected racing is, was Assistant Trainer to John Tilling during my time at Worstead's Farm (and, of course,

Michael went on to work for Vincent O'Brien and, as a trainer in his own right, handled the brilliant mare Kooyonga, winner of the 1992 Eclipse). It was a big blow losing so many good horses. Once again, just when things seemed to be coming right, bang, along came something to knock me back again.

Meanwhile, someone's come knocking at my door. Anthony Phillips. He just turned up, said he wanted to be an apprentice. I forget where he was from originally. Barbados or Jamaica. Anyway he was West Indian. We nicknamed him Rootsy after the TV series which was on then. He was a great kid. I never regretted taking him on. He rode work for me and did really well.

Having lost the McCaughey horses to Ireland, I started getting some new horses into the yard. Ironically, one of them was another Jim McCaughey owned horse, Fortune's Guest. That is a horse I will never, never forget. That horse was, in the worst sense of the word, an animal. He was a rogue. An absolute rogue. He was with Michael Stoute when I first heard of him. The Travelling Head Lad there, Jimmy Scott, was someone who I had met while I had still been an apprentice. We were – and still are – good friends. He told me that there was nothing that they could do with him, largely because they just couldn't devote enough time to him. He was, it seemed, a horse which was going to need a lot of attention given to him. Jimmy suggested that I should take him on. I decided to give it a go. Why not?

I didn't know what I was letting myself in for. Fortune's Guest was stubborn, lazy . . . a born trouble-maker. He didn't want to go anywhere. He wouldn't go out onto the road unless it was to lash out at any cars which were there. He wouldn't eat properly; would try and bite anyone who went near him. An animal. He really tested my patience, that horse. In fact, he made me realise that I really did have some.

102

Another character came with Fortune's Guest. Two-legged this one. Simon Whitworth. He had been apprenticed to Michael Stoute. Right, I thought, I'll put these two together. They deserve one another. They seem to have arrived as a package, I'll make them one. And that's what I did. It worked brilliantly. The two of them struck up a really good relationship, won quite a few races.

He is a cracking jockey, Simon Whitworth. He was close to being champion apprentice while he was with me. He was as hot-tempered as he was gifted. I must have sacked Simon at least once a week. The rucks we had! Terrible. Sometimes I'd sack him, think that was the end of it and then his Dad would call me. Simon's sorry. Simon wishes he hadn't said this, done that. Will you have him back? I always did. The next week we'd have another row. You're sacked! Sod off! Eventually we solved some of the problems by having him live in, as it were. We converted the hayloft in the barn into a bedsit for him. Once he was living in on the job he seemed to settle down.

The summer of '82 brought quite a few problems. Not least for me. I was getting a lot of pain in the side of my head, didn't really complain about it as much as I should have done. Eileen then noticed a lump on the side of my neck. I thought it would go away but it didn't. It kept on getting bigger. I was still getting a lot of pain. I went to the hospital and it was discovered that I had a blocked saliva gland. I had a cyst there. It had to be removed. I didn't want to go into the hospital for the operation, I had had enough of hospitals, but Ray Chiarella threatened to pull Bajan Sunshine out of the John Beckett Maiden Stakes, a race he had been entered up for at Yarmouth, unless I did. So in I went. And then in went Bajan Sunshine, providing me with my fifth win of the season. In doing so he also broke a three month losing streak which the stable had been through. His jockey that day was Dermot Browne. Dermot had just come over from Ireland to ride for the

Dickinson stable. Only weeks before he had still been riding as an amateur in Ireland, where his father, of course, was a well-known trainer. We had been intending to fly him over for the ride after the Racing Editor on the *Daily Telegraph*, Tony Stafford, recommended him to us. Bajan Sunshine was his first winner in England. It was Bajan Sunshine's first win anywhere. It was fabulous. After that he went on to win at Folkestone, where he was again ridden by Dermot Browne. All the while we had been stepping him up in distance. From 10 furlongs, to 12, to 14, to 15. When he won at Lingfield he won over 2 miles. And he put up a really sound display. Trevor Rogers said afterwards that he would have won by half the track if he had concentrated on the job more. As it was he still came within a second and a half of the 2 mile track record. Finally the late Tony Murray won on the horse at Doncaster. After the race Tony told me that he thought that Bajan Sunshine was developing into a very useful stayer. That confirmed it for us; with four wins under his belt and having really come to himself as a three year-old, we realised that we really were onto something with Bajan Sunshine. He had run nine races in all by then and had never finished out of the money. The Cesarewitch really was looking like a definite possibility.

We then ran Bajan Sunshine in three races at Goodwood, a course which we didn't really think was ideally suited to him. First of all he ran in the Alycidon Stakes, where he finished last of four runners but was doing all of his best work in the closing stages. He then ran in the March Stakes, where he again finished fourth (behind Santella Man, Father Rooney and Zilos). Finally he ran in the Stonehill Handicap and finished second to King's College Boy. All of those were good races, but it was that last race which really made his chance in the Cesarewitch clear. He had carried 9st 12lb there. In the Cesarewitch he was due to carry the bottom weight of 7st 7lb. John Lowe

Mr. & Mrs. Zandona with Sunny Banks Angel after winning at Salisbury

My string at Epsom

Joe Mercer wins on Petit Realm at Sandown; she was my best ever two year old

A trainer's race at Kempton, 1984, I'm in the centre kneeling

had the ride and after having ridden him on the gallops he too was confident that he could win. When he was originally entered for the Cesarewitch he had been quoted at odds of 66–1. They had then dropped to 40–1. Before going for the Stonehill he had won the Epsom Stakes at Lingfield. Down they came to 20–1. After the Stonehill he was promoted to 16–1 joint-favourite for the race.

While all this is going on, I'm still in and out of hospital on a regular basis. Trouble was, the surgeons couldn't remove all of the cyst because it had grown too much, had spread towards my eye, my ear and so on. If they weren't careful and cut too much of it out the side of my face would drop. I had radiation treatment in Guildford. Horrible. Worse than the operations I'd had. And it was then that I started mapping out a bit of a touch for one of my horses, Pierrot August.

Pierrot August was owned by a syndicate of friends from the Croydon area. There were ten of them altogether. All plasterers, brickies, van drivers, chippies. Working lads. My brother-in-law, Mick Wales, was one of them. They had all chipped in to have this horse in training with me. I picked the horse up (again, out of a field) for them, so it was quite cheap and, of course, training fees weren't as high then as they are now. Anyway, they wanted to have it laid out for a race, have a bit of a gamble on it. That's what I did for them. I got the horse ready, got them to spread their bets around at various shops. I was still undergoing radiation treatment at Guildford when it ran so I actually listened to the race in a betting shop on the way home. It came in at 33–1. They all won at least £3,300. For them, that was big bucks. They loved it. They were drunk for a month. After that some of the boys decided that they wanted to go along to the races the next time the horse ran. The next race in which I had Pierrot August entered was at Doncaster. They decided to make a real outing of it, go up the night before, stay in a hotel. They even flew up there from Gatwick. They spared no expense whatsoever.

Unfortunately, Pierrot August ran like a pig at Doncaster. Some of the boys had to lie about where they had got on the train on their way back so that they could afford to pay for their tickets.

That Autumn was particularly eventful. On October 3rd Eileen gave birth to our daughter, Rebecca. A week later, completely out of the blue, Robert Sangster sent me a horse, a two year-old Rago Navarro filly called Christmas Ornament. Richmonds, the horse transporters, phoned me to say they were delivering the horse. I told them that they must have the wrong person. They then told me that Mr. Sangster had bought the horse at the Doncaster sales to be sent on to be trained by me. I had never spoken to Mr. Sangster but I promptly wrote a letter to him thanking him for the horse. It was quite a surprise getting it. A very pleasant surprise.

And then came the Cesarewitch.

Bajan Sunshine went off at 10–1. My heart was in my throat. I really thought he might win it. In the event he finished a ten length eighth. Willie Carson won the race on Mountain Lodge. But I was far from disappointed. I really did feel that if I could get him back for the race the following year, I could win it at the second time of asking.

1983 was another roller-coaster year for me, full of ups and downs. On the one hand Jim McCaughey had brought his horses back from Ireland. On the other, when we came to kick off the flat season that year, we had the virus. It wasn't until mid-August, when Amarone won at 33–1, that we had so much as a sniff of a winner. In July African Pearl had looked like landing the Magnet Cup at York, ridden by Dennis McKay. His bit broke and Dennis was left without reins. Willie Carson went on to win the race on Dick Hern's Bedtime.

But then we got our first jumper into the yard, the ex-

David Elsworth trained Duke of Dollis. On his first race, a novice hurdle at Plumpton, he won. My first National Hunt runner, a winner. Anthony Webber rode him. It was unbelievable. The following day Fortune's Guest won a staying race at Wolverhampton. It was as though some sort of jinx had been lifted. Fortune's Guest, ridden by Simon Whitworth, went on to win the Midland Cesarewitch at Warwick while the 'Duke' went on to win two more races. By then we had been hit by more bad news. Again, just when things were beginning to roll, Jim McCaughey decided that he was going to have to get out of racing; he couldn't afford it anymore. He started selling off his horses.

When Jim McCaughey went, we were in trouble. South Hatch Racing had collapsed. I had to get out of South Hatch. And it was then that Vasant Advani stepped in. He had four horses with me then, including Amarone. He suggested that he set me up somewhere else. In the meantime he bought up some more horses. Khalif was one, I remember. He bought Fortune's Guest too. And relatively cheaply; no one else wanted him.

By the time the 1983 Cesarewitch came around my future was really in doubt. It looked quite possible that I might even be forced into early retirement. At the same time though, I had three lively candidates for the race: Bajan Sunshine, Fortune's Guest and Duke of Dollis. If one of them could win the race for me it would mean that I could pay the rent and hang on for a little while longer in the hope that something else might come up. It would give me some breathing space. Bajan Sunshine was the one I was banking on, of course. Like everything else in the yard he had been coughing, had had a runny nose. But he had also had a bruised foot and after that an abscess. Coming up to the Cesarewitch he had only won one race – his last, the Westmoreland Handicap at Bath. But that had put him straight. I knew he was back on

111

form, that he could do it. As for his foot: I had sat up late into the night with him, applying poultices and so on. I knew that there wasn't a problem there anymore. I had got him right. Fortune's Guest was on form and was well handicapped (at 7st 9lb) and so too was the 'Duke' who I was running to set the pace for Bajan Sunshine.

Bryn's gone now, of course; being retained jockey to Jim Mccaughey, he went when Jim McCaughey went. A double blow. So now my principal jockey is Simon Whitworth. Thinking that he had the best chance of the three horses I'd entered for the Cesarewitch, he decided that he wanted to ride Fortune's Guest. Besides which, he was the only one who could ride the bastard. Alan MacKay came in for the ride on the 'Duke' and I booked Brian Rouse for Bajan Sunshine.

We were away.

Two days before the race, mainly for financial reasons, Ray Chiarella sold Bajan Sunshine. He thought I was dreaming, living in cloud cuckoo land, thinking that I was going to win the race with him. All the same, he took out a bit of insurance; he included a percentage of any prize money from the Cesarewitch in the purchase price.

The big day came.

Once again my heart was in my throat as the race went off. Could I win it the second time around? Of course I could. And I was going to. Interviewed before the race I didn't beat about the bush. I said Bajan Sunshine was a certainty, advised everyone to go out and back him straight away, whether they put on 5p or £500. They just had to back him. He was a good thing.

And he damned well was. Bajan Sunshine started making headway about four furlongs out. With two to go he's out in front. In the final furlong Popsi's Joy, ridden by Shaun Keighley, joins him. But then he rallies again, runs on to the line, wins by a neck. Contester, who finished like a train, came in third. Mayotte, who had led with three·

furlongs to go, came in fourth. Fifth was Fortune's Guest. He had looked as though he might win for a moment but in that very same moment he had blown up. Because of his wayward nature we just hadn't got enough work into him. He wasn't fit enough. Duke of Dollis finished fifteenth.

Bajan Sunshine's win was a lot closer than I would have liked it to have been but I still think that the horse let Popsi's Joy come to him and then went and beat him again. He was an idle bastard once he hit the front. It was a lot easier than it looked. He went to Martin Tate after his win; his new owner, Paul Green, having promised him the horse. There's no denying it; it was heartbreaking. Nobody in the yard got the chance to say well done, goodbye, anything. He was gone. Interviewed by Brough Scott after the race, and knowing that the horse was about to go, I was pretty emotional. It was a bit hard to take, winning your biggest race and then losing the horse who had landed it immediately afterwards. And not only that . . . in a fortnight's time I was going to lose my whole yard, house and home! I had to tell Brough Scott I didn't know where I'd be going after that.

And that had to be my main worry: keeping a roof over my head. Bajan Sunshine had thrown me a lifeline but I was still in it up to my neck. I was still going to have to sell off other horses, for instance, just to keep things going. I sold the 'Duke'. He went to Roddy Armytage.

When Vasant Advani first joined me as an owner the horses he had in training were horses that he had purchased. At the same time though he had two or three mares from which he was breeding his own stock. Now, two years on, those horses were ready to race. It seemed that we could help each other out. He could set me up elsewhere. I could train these horses for him. I wanted to train dual purpose horses so Lambourn seemed like the ideal destination. And then Eileen's father saw a place for sale. 'Near Down'. A stable which had previously been occupied both by Reg Akehurst and Patrick Haslam. He sent us the details and we sent them on to Mr. Advani. Mr. Advani then sent us over to Lambourn to have a look at the place. We liked it. He decided to buy it, to employ me there as a waged trainer. But before he could, we had to get out of South Hatch. We had to find a stop-gap, somewhere to go in the interim with the string of eight horses that were coming to Lambourn with us.

We found it: a small stud at Leatherhead, a little stepping stone onto my biggest stage yet.

NEAR DOWN AND TERRY RAMSDEN

Keston Stud was owned by a Mrs. Mears. It was a lovely set-up. Beautiful paddock. Beautiful house. Beautiful stables (all of the boxes indoors). Fabulous. It was a damned nice place. If it had had the facilities I had needed to train my horses, gallops and so on, I'm sure that Mr. Advani would have bought it instead of Near Down; as it happened Mrs. Mears wanted to sell it. It was because it was empty that we had been able to move in. Certainly I would have been quite happy there. But there weren't the facilities, so that was that. End of story.

Mrs. Mears was living in the house while I was there and I was renting the stables and the indoor school from her. Where was I living? In a caravan in the barn. With a couple of my staff. With Barnaby. With the cats, for God's sake. Eileen is off at her mother's with Robin and Rebecca. I thought it was a situation which would only last for a few weeks or so. In the end it lasted for a few months.

That lunatic Fortune's Guest soon got up to his old tricks while we were at Leatherhead. There was a round-about near the stud. One morning Rootsy was riding him past it. Fortune's Guest decided that he was going to get onto it, play Roy Rogers with him. He got right in the middle of this bloody roundabout, started rearing up, everything. It was about eight o'clock so the roads were quite busy. People were stopping their cars to have a look. They were cheering and clapping. They thought it was some sort of rodeo show or something. In the end there were tailbacks every which way, all because of Fortune's Guest. Crazy.

115

Eventually early in the New Year (1984) we move into Near Down. It had been left empty for quite a while so it was in a fairly run down state. It was musty, damp and so on, full of rotting straw. We had to put in a lot of work just to get it straight again. Eileen and I moved into the house there. It was like the House-That-Jack-Built; it had extensions here there and everywhere around what was basically a two-up, two-down cottage. But it was pleasant. We soon settled in. We felt at home, happy there. And what's more, in complete contrast to how things had been at Epsom, the racing community in Lambourn went out of their way to welcome us. That played a big part in it, certainly. We were invited to parties, barbecues, you name it. Celebrations when someone had had a winner. Dances. Functions. Brilliant. They'd joke with me about the clothes I'd gained a reputation for wearing. When we heard that you were coming here we thought, bloody hell, what's going on? They gave me a best turned out award. I even acquired a nickname: the Valley Peacock. They were all fabulous. All of them. The Winters. The Hendersons. The Gaselees. The Francomes. The Francis's. The Sherwoods. The Coles. The Hills. The Walwyns. All of them. Fabulous. Steve Smith Eccles became a particularly close friend. Here's a jockey I've admired for years. Suddenly we're best mates. You couldn't believe it. That winter there was a big freeze up. We ended up playing snooker together quite often. And I remember going skating with him on the pond at Burford too – him, me and a load of other people. We didn't have skates. We just went out there in our wellies. Someone tripped Steve up with a hockey stick. It was funny. He had come out onto the ice taking tiny little steps, hardly making any progress at all. Now he shoots right across it.

Back to Fortune's Guest. There was no getting away from Fortune's Guest at Lambourn. He really came into his own there. It was there that he really started causing

116

trouble, havoc, chaos. I'd secured Simon as my stable jockey but even he couldn't control Fortune's Guest when he decided that he wanted to act up. Rootsy struck up a fantastic relationship with the horse too. It was lovely to see. But he couldn't control him on such occasions either. There was nothing anybody could do once Fortune's Guest got it into his head to play silly buggers. The things that horse got up to! He'd go into people's gardens and eat their shrubbery. He'd see a flower he liked. I want it! In he'd go. In through the garden gate, have a look through the front window, eat the flower. Whoever was riding him just had to sit there, let him get on with it. It was the same when he was out on the roads. Sometimes he'd just stop, holding up the traffic in both directions. You could push him, kick him, whip him. It made not a bit of difference. It made no difference at all. He would just stand there. You could get off him, go home, have a cup of tea. It was only when he thought that he'd caused enough trouble that he would finally consent to walk on again. And out on the gallops! Jesus. He'd beat into other strings working on the Downs. I lost count of the number of times he would suddenly cut out of our string with Simon or Rootsy, take off with them. The thing was, he'd have seen a horse in the other string that he had decided he was going to have. He'd have singled it out. And he's off. There's no stopping him. He would beat into this other string, try to savage this horse – I'm having you – and then come back to us again. He'd go half a mile out of his way just to do that sort of thing.

Like me Fortune's Guest had sent his reputation ahead of him. People had heard about him. Watch out for this big chestnut bastard with a white face. But they still weren't prepared for him. He was worse than they had expected. One morning I got a phone call from Fred Winter. I was amazed; he said he wanted to buy him. Like a naive prat I began to wonder how much I might get for him.

"Oh no, I don't want to race him," Fred said. "I want to shoot the bastard!" Apparently he'd created havoc with his horses on more than one occasion too.

But if Eileen and I found that we really liked being in Lambourn, the icing on the cake was that we really got the horses firing as well. Right from the off. During the winter months I had kept them going at the stud, in the indoor school. They were really fit. The thing is, you just don't realise at first just how much work they do in a situation like that. Out on the Downs they might be worked over a straight mile. That looks like a decent piece of work. In an indoor school though you just have them going around in circles. It doesn't look like they're doing much. But they are. Each circuit might be near enough a furlong. And you're working them several times one way, several times the other. They've gone a lot further than if they'd been out on the gallops. They've cantered maybe two miles or more before you realise it. We had jumps in there too, to keep them happy, and they popped over those. They really did get a good work-out. And, as I say, it showed once they got on the racecourse. In my first season at Near Down I had fifteen winners. And that from a stock of only eighteen horses. It was a fantastic start.

One horse who didn't fire though was Mr. Sangster's Christmas Ornament. I gave him every opportunity but he just wasn't any good. There was nothing there. In the end I advised Mr. Sangster to get rid of him. He took my advice and did just that. And Christmas Ornament never did go on to show anything. I thought that I might get another horse from Mr. Sangster but it wasn't to be. But so it goes.

In any event, there were compensations. That terrific start in my first season at Near Down did succeed in attracting several other owners – including the renowned Terry Ramsden, a flamboyant businessman who had made his name – and his fortune – on the Japanese

118

warrant market and who was then one of the biggest gamblers on the scene. He already had a number of horses in training but he wanted to get involved with a good, small team which would help him set up a few touches. So he sent me a couple of horses – both from Peter Easterby's yard.

As I have already mentioned, Tony Stafford is Racing Editor on *The Daily Telegraph*. It was Tony who helped Simon Whitworth challenge for champion apprentice while I was at Epsom by steering him towards other rides from other stables. And during my first season at Near Down he was absolutely brilliant. It's no exaggeration to say that, fit though the horses were, I would never have had fifteen winners if it hadn't been for him. He understood the handicapping system inside out. He taught me that you shouldn't run with certain penalties, how to use weight allowances and apprentices to your advantage. He really did help me that first season. He helped me a lot as he has helped many people in racing.

It seemed then that it really was all systems go. I had secured Simon as my stable jockey. I had secured several winners. My future looked secure (or as secure as it ever can be in racing). I had the horses in, I wasn't having to worry about the property . . . I wasn't having to worry about anything. Everything looked rosy at last. But then, once again, I ran straight into a brick wall. Just when I thought that I might finally have cracked it, bang, I'm in trouble again. Suddenly Mr. Advani has to pull out. Like Mr. McCaughey before him, he's got financial problems. His horses have to go. Fortune's Guest went. Through connections which Simon had made there during the winter, he went to stud in India. All of Mr. Advani's horses went. It was terrible.

I looked to be on the rocks again. Until Terry Ramsden stepped in. He decided to buy the yard, rent it to me – provided that I could keep sufficient horses there to make it feasible. And that was the nice thing about Terry Ramsden; the first thing he did was make sure that, once we had done our paperwork, the rent was beneath what we could afford to pay. Saved.

French-horses were then a relatively untapped resource as far as British trainers were concerned so when Terry Ramsden decided that he wanted some new horses, over we went. And we got some really nice animals there. Some (like Hogmany who, of course, eventually turned out to be a top-class chaser) we had to turn down; Terry wanted horses which were ready to run. That was all that we were interested in. We weren't buying stock for the future. We wanted to run our purchases straight away. So a company was set up, Excite Ltd., for the horses to run under. This meant, of course, that the horses that Terry Ramsden had in training with me started running under different colours. Red with a blue cap with white spots instead of the old blue and white. It wasn't long before the bookies twigged what was going on but it gave us a bit of an advantage for a while and we made the most of it; landed a few nice touches with horses like Pinctada and Grand Celebration. Up until then any Terry Ramsden horse automatically had its price clipped. The horses were only winning small races, sellers and so on, but they were winning a lot of them. It was a good time.

I really enjoyed the Excite connection. We would fly over to France to be met by a bloodstock agent and then we would go to all the big yards, studs and so on. We went to the Aga Khan's stud. And he has what are probably the best bloodlines in the world. We met Criquette Head, bought horses from her (Temperance Way, for example).

After a while John Francome started going over with me. John had just started training then. He would ride and school the horses. It was great to watch. John was – and still is – such a good jockey. "Let's canter that one,

John," I'd say. "Let's hack that one down." On he'd get and off they'd go. We went to yards all over the shop, moved from one on to the next. Maison Lafitte. Chantilly. Everywhere. We'd bought a cine-camera, filmed all the horses. When we got back to Lambourn we would go over everything. We'd decide which horses we liked. And then we might phone to arrange another trip over to France the following week. Listen, we don't like that one, we like this one. Can we come back out again maybe Monday or Tuesday? We'd like to have another sit on him and then we'll make a decision. At five o'clock in the morning there we'd be at Gatwick. Over the Channel we'd go. John would ride out on a few more horses. We'd film them. We'd buy the ones we'd decided we liked. We'd buy three, four, five or six in any one batch. We might have to buy some rubbish as part of the deal but we would also get some good horses. One nice horse which John got was Castaglione. I got horses like Brunico, Star's Delight, Mausolee and Santopadre. Each one might cost £5,000 – £20,000 but we'd put together a package for, say, £50,000. When I got them home people like Fred Winter might phone me up. Rodney, Fred Winter here. I've just been reading in the paper about these new horses you've got. Any chance of popping over after breakfast to have a look? Fabulous days. Long gone now I'm afraid. Now any number of trainers have bought French-bred horses. Jenny Pitman. Charlie Brooks. Oliver Sherwood. Henrietta Knight. Martin Pipe. The prices have shot up. I can't afford to buy horses there anymore. I haven't got that sort of owner.

While all this was going on Tony Stafford bought a 3,400 guineas horse from the sales. Tangognat. He had wanted something that could be put away for a year, come out as a three year-old to run on the flat and then turn to novice hurdling. At first he took a bit of stick for going to Tangognat. The horse had exceptionally long pasterns which meant

121

that it would only go on very soft ground, but he was adamant that it would prove to be a decent horse. And he was right.

I remember a horse called Caliph winning for me that season. He was a strange animal. At home he was quite savage, was always trying to kick people, bit them. On the racecourse he always seemed to think that he had to give every other horse at least a hundred yard start. And in sprint races too! I used to ask jockeys to give him a crack with the whip as soon as they left the stalls to try and get him to keep up with the pace a bit more – but he wouldn't. He kept on getting beaten. Until, that is, Lester Piggott rode him in a race at Sandown. Once again Caliph wouldn't stay up with the pace. That didn't bother Lester though. With a little more than two furlongs of the race left he seemed to be falling asleep on Caliph. He wasn't moving a muscle, he was still in mid-division then. No-where. With a furlong to go a horse called His Dream was clear, looked like he had the race in the bag. Suddenly Lester got Caliph going. It was astonishing to see. They flew past everything. And they flew past His Dream, won by a neck. It's no wonder people get so worked up about Lester Piggott. He really is a very, very special jockey. He's a one-off.

The 1985 season was as bad as the 1984 season had been good, the main reason being that the stable was hit by a prolonged virus. Winners were just very difficult to come by. We only had nine winners in all. It was damned frustrating.

In that second season Simon Whitworth left to join Kim Brassey's yard. Kim ad a string of 40–50 horses and when the vacancy came up there it was just too good an opportunity for him to pass up. Rootsy left too – to go and ride in Canada. I got in a new apprentice, a Liverpool lad called Kevin Radcliffe. He wasn't really cut out to be a jockey but he worked hard. The following year he rode Tony

Stafford's Tangognat to two good wins. First of all, at 20–1, he won the Ruth Wood Maiden Stakes at Kempton by twenty lengths. Ten days later we went back there for the Magnolia Stakes. He won that by fifteen lengths, this time going off at 6–5. After that he was put away to reappear as a hurdler.

One other thing which I remember from those early years at Near Down was the night our barn burned down. The fire was caused by spontaneous combustion in some hay and straw. It was Eileen who first noticed it. There was a craze in Lambourn for remote-controlled model cars at the time and she was making one in the kitchen. By the time the fire brigade got out to us the barn was completely ablaze. It only took a few minutes to turn into a proper inferno. The roof, which was made of corrugated iron, was just exploding into the air. These huge sheets were spinning off every which way. It was terrible. The horses coped with it all pretty well though. We usually had quite loud music on in the yard so perhaps with all the blue lights flashing and everything they thought that they were in a nightclub. Anyway we moved those which were nearest the barn. They seemed none the worse for it all. Later that night the fire brigade had to come back for a second time when the fire flared up again. I remember too that people were really supportive of us after the blaze. It underlined, again, just how welcoming people in Lambourn were towards us. In no time at all Simon Sherwood was on the phone offering us the use of some of the boxes in his yard if we needed them. In fact, the whole of Lambourn seemed to be queuing up to help. They had seen the blaze in the darkness, turned up with horse-boxes, phoned up offering boxes in their stables, offered me straw and hay to replace what I'd lost. It was lovely. I was inundated with offers of help. I was quite over-whelmed by it all.

Terry Ramsden. He wasn't a man of many words, but

he got things done. Yeah, here's a horse. Yeah, just send me the bill. Rod, let's meet, I'll send a taxi over for you. I found him easy to get on with. Easy. Our association lasted for about three years and we were really quite successful. He had his best horses with Jenny Pitman. The best horse he had with me was probably Mausolee. Unfortunately, that was another good horse of mine that was killed. It got loose on the gallops one day, ran home and ran straight into a brick wall. Smack. Gone. Horses just do that sometimes. They get loose and they just run and run. He was a big baby, Mausolee. But he had a lot of class. He could have been anything. He won a couple of decent races and won them cosily.

As Terry gained confidence in me he began to go for quite a few gambles on some of the horses I was training for him. Of course, we've all read in the papers that he's said to have gambled away something like £77 million during the 80's and I'm sure that he must have lost some of that backing those horses. Terry Ramsden definitely went for some big touches. But quite often he would turn to me to win his money back for him after he had had a gamble turned over at some other stable. And I landed several good gambles for Terry Ramsden. Cool Enough. It's now in training with Linda Ramsden. Still winning. It had no real form. It had bad knees. But we set it up for a one-off gamble first time out in a selling race at Thirsk. It was Simon's first ride for Terry. It won. We landed similar touches with Pinctada, an Excite horse which came to me after being with Wilf Storey initially. We landed another nice touch with Fiefdom – who is also still in training, ironically, with Wilf Storey, still winning his share of races.

If 1985 had started badly, with all of my horses sickening with the virus, 1986 couldn't have got off to a better start. On New Year's Day Tangognat won the Steel Plate Trial Hurdle at Cheltenham, so confirming all of his earlier

124

promise. It was quite a pick-me-up as far as I was concerned. Just before Christmas I had gone into Nuffield Orthopaedic Hospital. My leg had been giving me quite a lot of pain, the surgeons decided that it needed to be broken and reset. You can imagine how that made me feel. Some Christmas present. At the same time they decided to operate on my bunions (the result of wearing wellington boots twenty four hours a day while I was working as a stable lad). I spent Christmas on crutches, was still having to use them when I went to Cheltenham. But once I saw Tangognat quicken up the hill there I forgot all about the fact that I was hobbling along on crutches again, forgot all about what a miserable time I'd had for the previous twelve months. Gone. And Tony Stafford was well pleased too. After the race Tangognat was made 8–1 favourite for the Triumph Hurdle. He had backed it at 50–1.

And things got better still. After the Steel Plate Tangognat went on to win the Bet With The Tote Hurdle in which he was ridden by Peter Scudamore. Meanwhile I've got another horse which looks as though it could be a Triumph contender. Brunico. I bought the horse from the Egyptian-born French trainer Maurice Zilber. It had only won one race in France but I knew that it was good, that it could turn out to be more than useful. Whereas Tangognat was pretty much an out-and-out stayer, Brunico was also blessed with an exceptional turn of foot. He was a grey too. I like greys. If I haven't got one in the yard I'll always be tempted to go out and buy one. I think they're lucky. Terry Ramsden bought the horse. We worked it with Tangognat and there really wasn't anything to choose between the two of them. When Brunico made his debut at Windsor on January 15th 1986, he was 'expected'. He went off as 7–4 favourite for the Rays Novices Hurdle there and, ridden by Dermot Browne, duly obliged.

A big freeze-up interrupted my (everyone's) preparations for Cheltenham. To keep Brunico and Tangognat in trim I took them to Burnham-on-Sea near Weston-Super-Mare and galloped them on the beach there. I must have worked them there three or four times.

And suddenly it's Triumph day. And as happens so often in racing nothing went to plan. Tangognat injured himself so badly during the race that he was pulled up, never raced again. It was a fluke, a freak accident. A shaft of wood from one of the hurdles went up the inside of his near fore brushing boot, gave him a really nasty gash, badly damaged his tendons. It was a serious injury. It finished his racing career just as it was starting. Brunico suffered his own particular bad luck. Coming to the final hurdle he must have been all of thirty lengths behind the leader, the 33–1 shot Solar Cloud. On the hill he really got stuck in though, put all of his finishing speed to use. But he just couldn't quite get to the winner. He came in a fast-finishing second.

Never mind. There's always another day. And come the Chester May meeting Brunico did his work on the flat. I'll never forget it. We went for the Group 3 Ormonde Stakes with him. Five years before in May 1981 Billbroker had been pipped at the line by the Michael Stoute trained favourite Pelerin. Now I get my revenge. Brunico, helped by the ground having come up soft, got up ahead of Michael's Shadari, the 6–5 on favourite for the race. He won by 1½ lengths at 33–1 ridden by Brent Thompson. My first Group winner. It was a fantastic moment. I was so pleased that I punched Terry Ramsden's 32-stone minder. I was ecstatic.

Brunico went on to win (narrowly) at Sandown and (on the flat, ridden by Tim Thomson Jones) at Doncaster. Eventually he became a leading contender for the 1987 Champion Hurdle. Unfortunately he never got to the race. He started 'thinking' too much. He flopped in the Princess Royal Handicap Hurdle where he had been made an

126

evens favourite, coming in a 16 length fourth to Mercy Rimell's Bel Course, was taken out of the betting. Graham McCourt, who rode him that day, described him as being a 'bit mulish'. Called on for an effort in the home straight he ducked away from the whip, veered about all over the shop. Before the race he had even been a bit reluctant to go down to the start. It was very disappointing. I watched the camera patrol film several times and he just looked a different horse to the one who had won the Ormonde. There was no way that he was going to be able to go for the Champion if this was a sign of things to come. And, unfortunately, it was. Brunico went downhill, never even looked like winning afterwards. He had the ability all right; it was his attitude that was the problem. In the end it became obvious that we were going to have to take him out of the game altogether. Eventually we sold him to a Dorsetshire dairy farmer, to go point-to-pointing. He then sold him to Ron Hodges. But still Brunico was proving impossible to win with. So he went back to point-to-pointing with another owner. And now look what's happened. The old devil's won eight on the trot, looks as though he might reach the record of straight point-to-point wins (which currently stands at 11, I think I'm right in saying). Obviously he's still got all of his old ability . . . and now, at long last, he's choosing to show it again. Good luck to him.

It was shortly before Brunico's Doncaster flop that I got a new apprentice: Dean Gallagher, whose father, Tom Gallagher, was Travelling Head Lad to Jim Bolger in Ireland. His cousin, Mark, had been with me for about a year and a half by then. Mark won his first race for me on Harrison at Brighton. He won on Hendryk at Bath. On Pinctada at Lingfield. He rode some good winners for me. But then he got an offer to ride in Macau. Dean replaced him.

Dean's first ride for me was on a horse called Rymoss at Bangor. It was a disaster. Rymoss decided that he didn't want to run that day, went only so far and then ducked out through the rails to get back to the stables again. On March 2nd Brunico disappointed at Doncaster. The following day Dean rode his first winner for me. He rode Harbour Bazaar in the Coombe's Handicap Hurdle at Plumpton. It was a gratifying win for another reason too. It meant that all but one of the ten jumpers which I then had in training had won – the one exception, of course, being the enigmatic, exasperating Brunico.

I've never been a big gambler myself. Shortly before Eileen and I got married I had £980 in a building society account. Ken Payne, for whom I did a lot of work at Prior's Court, of course, had a horse that he thought couldn't get beaten. Button Boy it was called. Johnny Curant was riding it. I put £950 on it. Win. It lost. But now the situation's different. I'm training. And things are going well. I'm never tempted to have a bet when things are going badly. If the money isn't in the pot, don't play. That's the rule I try to stick to. With things going so well at Near Down though I was tempted on numerous occasions. It was all due to my own hard work. I had put heart and soul into the horses. Why not a bit of cash? I had a bet on a few occasions, but I'm not talking a lot of money here. Usually I didn't get involved, left that side of things to Terry and Tony.

If I had joined in with some of the big gambles we pulled off in those days I'd probably be a rich man by now. I knew when my horses were going to win. I knew they were certainties. I knew. Once, when I was at Folkestone, I took a chair into the winner's enclosure after the horses had gone down to the start. Everyone thought I was crazy. The thing was though, I didn't want to have a bet, I just wanted to wait for my horse to come back. And that's what I did. I didn't even watch the race from the stands. I just sat there and waited for it. It won.

A while later I did the same thing at Chester. And then

at Sandown on Variety Day. On that occasion, I remember, I was running another of Terry's horses, Valued Collection, in a seller. That won too. But then as soon as it came into the winner's enclosure it started bucketing down. There was a real downpour. Everyone ran for cover. I grabbed my chair and went with them. The auction was called off. As soon as the rain stopped though they decided to go ahead with it after all. I had to go to £9,000 to buy the bugger back. And then I started getting really cocky. Before Bajan Sunshine won the Cesarewitch I had played up to the Press quite a bit, telling them that he wouldn't get beaten.

"What if it rains?"

"Yeah."

"What if you get iced-up?"

"Yeah."

"What if the horse gets an injury?"

"Yeah. He can be lame and win this. He can fall over and win this. The jockey can get off, get on every other horse in the race, get back on and still win. He's going to win."

Now I'm not only predicting when my horses are going to win though. Oh no. Now I'm predicting by how many lengths. I'm really going for it. The Press loved it, of course, And it all added to my image too; the colourful quotes went well with the colourful clothes. It got me noticed. But, as I've said before, that was only part of it. It was also just a lot of fun. It was a laugh.

Terry thought it was funny at first. But then he got a bit annoyed about it because he thought I was giving too much away. He gave me a right bollocking about it once. Mind, I thought that was a laugh too. And so did he in the end. It was all just part of the crack. End of story.

Less amusing was an incident that took place at Cheltenham on Triumph Hurdle day when Brunico and Tangognat were running. It was a cold, wet, miserable day and we were standing in the ring. Suddenly the police came up to us. Mr. Ramsden, we're afraid that a death threat has been made against you. There's supposed to be this sniper somewhere trying to shoot him. We all had to go off, come back into the ring again wearing bullet-proof vests. Crazy. Frightening too. I've worn some strange things, I know . . . but a bullet-proof vest!

Terry always had bodyguards. He used to have too many, I think. Sometimes they would be swarming around him. I think he felt sorry for them; would rather give them a job than see them end up in jail.

It was in 1986 that I went to Florida for a few weeks. I just wanted to find out what the scene was like over there. Bloodstock agents from Florida were forever coming around the small yards looking for horses to race there, it just sparked my interest. The owner of Secreto, that year's Derby winner, lived in Florida and I took a framed photo of the horse winning the race over to him. I stayed in the Holiday Inn near Calder Racecourse, spent a lot of time with the racehorse trainer Charlie Stutts who trained nearby. I loved it over there. Loved it. I loved all the razzmatazz. It was fabulous. If I had been given the chance to train over there I would have taken it like a shot. Wouldn't have thought twice about it. As it was I just brought a little bit of the Florida racing scene back with me. I came back with all sorts of brightly coloured nosebands and bandages for my horses to wear. And I mean bright. They were neon orange. Neon green. Neon red. We won quite a few best turned-out when I first started putting them on my runners. Now, of course, things have become much more conservative again and that sort of thing is frowned upon. I don't run the horses in them very much anymore.

What else did we get up to? We tried to make Pinctada Horse of the Year in 1987, I remember that well. It was a competition which William Hill used to run to see which horse could win the most races in a season. We thought

Pinctada could do it. And in the end we went damn close. We were right up there, but got pipped by Chaplin's Club. We tried to get all the wins on the trot too. Ten of them. That's what we went for. Tony thought that if we could stay on the right side of the handicapper we could do it. He thought it was possible. So off we went. We won six on the trot. Twice at Doncaster. Twice at Lingfield. Once at Beverley. Once at Brighton.

We used Simon Whitworth first time out, claimed an allowance. That was at Beverley on May 11th. And his win there got me off the mark for the season. Until then I had been having some appalling luck. Lots of my horses were sidelined. Trouble was, too many of my jump horses were also my flat horses. They needed to have a break some-time. Those that were running were just getting touched off, Pinctada included. And to make matters worse I had lost two good horses within three days of each other: a good filly of Terry's shattered her pelvis at Chester and then I lost another at Bath. Pinctada enabled us to put all that behind us, thank God. Simon had been pushing him along from a fair way out but once he hit the front with two furlongs to go, and despite the fact that he was tiring, he was never really in danger. He won by 2½ lengths over Highland Image.

We then went to Lingfield. May 20th. Tim Thomson Jones rode him in an amateurs' race (no penalty for the winner). Pinctada came through in the final furlong to win by a length.

May 23rd and we're at Brighton (where Mark Gallagher had won on Harrison the previous day – his first winner for me). Simon rode him again. Pinctada was always going well in the race, had a comfortable ½ length to spare over Silver Form at the line.

May 26th and we went back to Lingfield. Another handicap race (Pinctada was still only on 8st 3lb). Mark Gallagher rode. Pinctada took up the running two furlongs out, held his nearest pursuer, Sergeant Meryll, by three lengths. That gave him a score of three wins within a week, four within 15 days. Quite an achievement.

After that we had to put the horse away for a while, sort out a few niggling problems, make sure that he was still fit enough to do himself justice. He reappeared again on July 2nd at Doncaster. Simon rode him again. He won again.

But then the ground came against us. It came up firm. Everywhere. There was just no way that I could safely run the horse. Our attempt on the ten-timer went out of the window.

We managed to slip in a sixth win though. Again at Doncaster. Mark Gallagher won on him in another apprentices' race.

We worked the system. And all this with a horse who was extremely difficult to keep sound, who had brittle knees and joints (which was why he couldn't run on firm ground). We were disappointed not to get the ten, disappointed to be beaten by Chaplin's Club who, I think I'm right in saying won seven races on the trot, but even so. It was a hell of an effort. And Pinctada went on to win plenty more good races too. In 1988 he won the Bunbury Cup, finished second in the race the following year. He was a smashing horse. I loved him. And so did a lot of other people. Because of the problems he had, because of the success he had in spite of them, he gained quite a following did that little terrier.

Just to go back to the subject of backing horses again: a man once came up to me at a meeting where Pinctada was running. He was a complete stranger. He asked me how well the horse was. "If you think the horse is well," he said. "I've got £50,000 that says he's too good for this lot." I told him that Pinctada was well and with that he pulled £50,000 in cash out of this bag, handed the lot over to a bookmaker, took odds of 6–4. I was amazed. Jesus, I thought, what if the horse over-reaches on the way down to the start? What if the saddle slips? What if it spreads a plate? All the sorts of things I worried about when Terry or Tony had had a big bet. But at least they had a direct line to the horses. This bloke didn't. £50,000! The responsibility really hit me. What if he had a family, had hocked house, home and goods just to get out of trouble? I didn't even know if the horse was spot on. I hadn't worked him for three days. As it worked out though Pinctada never looked like losing, won again. I never saw the man again.

Lashkafdal was an interesting horse that Terry bought. He bought the horse, a son of Shergar, from the Aga Khan to send it hurdling. Lashkafdal was a funny old character. He was a bit temperamental. Classy, but temperamental. He was a bit snooty. If he wanted to run he would. If he didn't he wouldn't. End of story. He won at Warwick, was placed twice and then went for the Mecca Bookmakers Novice Handicap at Sandown. The handicapper gave him an impossible 12–3lb. I put up a conditional jockey, Vivian Kennedy, to take some of the weight off. It made no difference. The boy didn't really give the horse a good ride, as I'm sure he'd admit. He overdid the waiting tactics and ended up getting tailed off. We got brought before the stewards over it. I remember Vivian kept jumping up and down next to me. "What's the matter with you?" I asked him. "I'm standing next to the fire and I'm burning," he said. It probably prepared him for the roasting I was about to give him. Sadly, Lashkafdal was another good horse that I lost through extremely unfortunate circumstances. He got a cut in his leg, near the knee. Nothing. It was a minor injury. The vet gave him a shot of antibiotics. What happened? He reacted against the injection and an infection set in. There was nothing that we could do about it. Because he continued to react against all of the antibiotics which we gave him he just got worse and worse and worse. In the end he had to be put down. It was terrible blow losing him because of something like that. It was a terrible blow losing him for any reason. He could have been a very, very good horse, Lashkafdal.

Terry Ramsden and I had some good times together. Fabulous times. The kids got in on the act too. Sometimes my secretary, Mary, would come in. *Terry's coming down. He'll be here about ten o'clock. Can you put a marker out in the paddock?* He'd fly straight into the paddock in his helicopter. They loved it, would run out there to sit in it. Terry would then come in – Hello, boys. How are you? –have a cup of tea and a chat, look over the horses.

But when those good times came to an end they came to an end with a real bang. Terry's company, Glen International, fell victim to the 1987 stock market crash. Once Terry had been listed the 57th richest person in the country. He gambled – and lost – millions. Between 1980 and 1987, as we all know by now, he's supposed to have lost something like £100 million. That he could sustain such losses indicates just how wealthy he was. When the crash came though, that was it. Glen International's collapse wiped him out.

As soon as Terry realised that he was in trouble, he told me. He was open with me right from the start. He wasn't like one of these people who might say, Rod, keep the horses and then go on to run up a bill they couldn't pay. "Get rid of them," he said. "Tell me how much I owe you." He didn't have to do that. He could have kept me in the dark, kept the horses with me. He had ten horses with me then. At £1,000 per horse per month the fees soon mount up.

So we sold them all. All of his horses. Brunico. Santopadre. Star's Delight. The Grand National hope, Stearsby, which Terry had moved to me from Jenny Pitman's yard. The lot. We cleared the account. I was left with ten empty boxes. And that was my relationship with Terry Ramsden over. Gone. And then, of course, Ladbrokes took Terry to the Tattersall's Committee when he defaulted on a gambling debt of £2 million – a figure which would once have seemed quite paltry to him. The Jockey Club warned him off. That really was the end. In the two and a half years or so that we had been working together I had trained 38 winners for him from 25 horses.

Meanwhile, I had other problems on my plate. Terry had asked me if I wanted to buy Near Down from him when he realised that he was going under and, after taking some advice on the matter, I had done. That was the biggest mistake I've ever made. I'll regret it to the day I die. The purchase price was £300,000 – which was what Terry had originally paid for it. I started off paying something like £1,800 a month on the mortgage, having borrowed the whole £300,000. But then the mortgage rates went up. Originally it had been 10%. Now it was 12%. Now it was 12.5%. The repayments were nearing £2,500 a month once it went up to 14%. And this while I've got half the boxes in the yard empty. That Flat season (1988) I managed to gain 8 winners. During the '88 – '89 N.H. season I managed to gain three more. The 1989 Flat ended with me having 7 winners (at York, Newcastle, Wolverhampton, Leicester, Sandown and, twice, at Brighton). I struggled on.

Sometimes when things start going badly though, they just don't stop. Instead, they pile up on one another. And that's what happened to me. When I was still reeling from this latest crisis in my life, my father died. Just before Christmas 1989 he had a heart attack. He went into hospital. I went over to see him. Almost as soon as I got back home again afterwards I got a phone call from my mother to say that he had suddenly taken a turn for the worse. When I got back to the hospital he had recovered again. He seemed all right. I went home for a second time. Everyone thought that he was out of danger. No worries. He died that night. I was upset for a very, very long time. I felt that we had never shared enough time together. I had wanted him to be there during all my good times, all my bad times. But all too often his work had got in the way. Mine had. It was one of those no-win situations. And, of course, even if he'd had more time, I couldn't expect him to have devoted it all to me anyway. Paul had needed a lot of attention after his accident, for instance. Later, Mary had had a very difficult pregnancy and she needed my mother and father's support.

A couple of years ago I was driving home from the races at Nottingham. It was June, but it was absolutely belting down. I had one of my owners with me. Suddenly I got this real sense of my father. I had to stop the car, get out. I stood there in the rain in tears.

Early 1990. The interest rate is now 16.5%. It just didn't look as though it was ever going to stop going up. It was just getting higher and higher. It really was frightening. Terrifying. And then it went up to 17%. In the end I was paying £3,500 a month on the mortgage – getting on for twice what I had originally been paying. Crazy. Well, it was easy to work out wasn't it? We were going bankrupt. We were going under, no two ways about it. It was a terrible time then. Terrible. Everything had turned very, very sour. I was depressed, angry, bitter. My marriage suffered. My health suffered. Everything suffered. I felt like packing it all in, getting out, giving it all up. But I couldn't. I couldn't even do that. I couldn't sell the damned place. I had been trying to do that from the very first moment the interest rates went up. It was hopeless. No one wanted to buy in that economic climate. Meanwhile, there were no new horses coming in, things were getting worse and worse and worse. In the end I had no choice other than to cease trading. I had to think of my family. I put my company, Rod Simpson Racing Ltd., into voluntary liquidation, had the yard rented out to me. The Jockey Club said that they would grant me a licence to carry on training but I knew that I had to be realistic, face the possibility that I finally might be forced out of racing. So I asked them to renew my licence for another two months, review the situation after that. And that's what they did. While all this had been going on I had been hoping to move to Delamere Stables, a nearby yard which had once been occupied by Ray Laing. It had been on the market for two years, had been vacant all that time. It would have been ideal for me. It was about half the size of Near Down. Perfect. But, of course, the economic climate then tied everyone's hands. No one could buy anywhere else because they couldn't sell what they already had. My problem was that I couldn't afford to buy it. Unless I could sell Near Down I had to move to somewhere that I could rent. The whole plan fell through. In the end I think it was Tom McGovern who moved into Delamere.

I was so frustrated. It looked hopeless. It really did look as though I was going to be forced out of racing. But then what would I do? Run a hotel perhaps? I've always thought that I'd like to do that. But where was the money going to come from? Retire to the house in Cornwall for a while, get a small job down there? In fact I actually applied for a job there I was so desperate. Didn't get it. Go to Macau, Arabia, Australia, the USA? Would that be fair on my family though, the kids especially? And, of course, I would need to be invited, to have someone backing me. I didn't have that. The fact was, I didn't really know what else I wanted to do . . . what else I could do. I knew what I wanted to do. I wanted to carry on doing what I was doing. I told the Press that I would continue training "even from a pig farm in the Outer Hebrides" if I had to. And I meant it. If it meant that I could carry on training I would do it.

But if I was going out, I was going out fighting. On March 17th 1990 Rouyan, who had earlier run a good race to be third behind Silver King in the Stroud Green Hurdle at Newbury and again to be second to Regal Lake in the Swish Hurdle at Chepstow, won the Northern Champion Juvenile Hurdle at Newcastle at 7–1. Ridden by Billy Morris he came home 2½ lengths ahead of Philosophus having taken up the running at the final flight. It was just the sort of win I needed. Not least because I had backed him to win. I'd had him spot on for the Chepstow race and had backed him then but the ground as just too soft for him. I recovered all of my losses from that and more besides. Torius won at Sandown at 33–1, ridden by Simon Whitworth. "Rod's Reprieved" said one of the newspaper headlines the next day after I had described myself as feeling like a man standing on a very shaky chair with a rope around my neck. Shortly afterwards he then won the Rookery Claiming Stakes at Sandown at 10–1, again ridden by Simon Whitworth ("Simpson Refuses To Fade Away!").

We struggled on, notched up 6 winners during that Flat season (Millfields Lady won twice, so too did Besito and Torius. Xhai won once) . . . but then the Halifax Building Society gave us our eviction notice. We had to be out of Near Down by November 7th. But by then I had another straw to clutch at. Fox Hill Farm, a yard near Wanborough, six miles outside Lambourn, became available – for rent. Years earlier part of the farm had been a training yard but it had all been allowed to go. The stables had been turned into cowsheds, the gallops had been ploughed up by the M4. But now a new owner, who had inherited the farm, had come in, had decided to convert it back to its former status. He put in some gallops, cleared the cows out . . . cleared the way for a trainer to move in. It was still a shambles. But then so was everything else in my life then. Why not, I thought. It was just what I wanted. I could soon get the place up and running (and the horses too). It offered me an opportunity to get out of Near Down, make a clean break of it and start again. And that was what I decided to do. I decided to cut my losses at

Near Down and just get out. Go. I arranged for us to move on to Foxhill. The last winner that I turned out from Near Down was Stage Player. In October he won the Salmon Spray Challenge Trophy Hurdle at Fontwell at 8–1, ridden by Billy Morris. "In Tune Player Lifts Gloom for Simpson" read a headline in one of the newspapers afterwards. In fact the gloom was already lifting. By then I had already begun preparing for the move to Foxhill.

Everything went through without a hitch. We spent Christmas 1990 in our new home.

Against all the odds I had survived. Just. But once again I was back at square one, having to start from scratch rather than being able to build on what I had already achieved. And that was why I decided to name the new yard Deja-Vu.

I had been through it all before.

HORSES AND COURSES

I wouldn't really say that I have a favourite racecourse as such. I think, as a trainer, that your favourite course is simply wherever you happened to have your last winner. Beyond that you're thinking of those courses which have generally been good to you. For me, that's Chester. It's a beautiful course. I've had some disasters there though. When I went there for the May meeting in 1991 I lost one of my best (and favourite) horses, Pinctada. He injured himself during the race, had to be put down the following day. But on the whole the good times far outnumber the bad at Chester. I had my first group winner there, of course. Brunico. In addition, Chester is quite simply a great place to go. It's a beautiful town. The racecourse is first class.

I like Brighton. It's a nice little track that they have there. It's a gaff track, sure; it doesn't have the facilities that would make it otherwise. But I like it. I rode there when I was an apprentice and I've had quite a few winners there since, so it's always been a bit special for me. In fact, I like small seaside tracks in general. Simple as that. I like Folkestone. Yarmouth. They have a good atmosphere about them. They're fun.

Goodwood. Now there's a strange racecourse. They've spent too much money on the stands in my opinion, not enough on the actual track. Because of that it attracts the crowds rather more than it does trainers. You never get quite as many runners as you might expect at Goodwood. But having said that, I like Goodwood. It's beautifully situated and I enjoy going there.

140

Winter 1985, Near Down, I'm on the grey

The Sporting Life's Monty Court with the "last of the mohicans" at Ascot !

Rouyan, ridden by Bill Morris, comes in at Sandown after winning the £25,000 Tote Jackpot Handicap Hurdle in 1991

Working for the corporate entertaining company Cavendish I enjoy a joke at Goodwood with R.S.M. Scott of the Kings Own Borderers

I like York. York is an exceptionally good racecourse. I wish I had horses of sufficient quality to run there more often. They look after you at York too. If you're a trainer who's gone to York, you get a free lunch. They encourage you to race there. They make you feel welcome. Some racecourses seem to say don't bother coming. It's exemplary, York. The way it's run, the facilities, the track. The lot.

Newbury. The owner and trainer are well catered for at Newbury now that the rebuilding work there has been completed. It's a good course for racegoers and for the horses too. It can be a difficult course to get in and out of though.

Another course which I particularly like is Sandown. Like York, it's a course where they've got things right across the board. They've worked damned hard there and it shows.

I also like Kempton. That's a good course. Chepstow too. Chepstow has the potential to be absolutely top-flight. It's one of the best now, don't get me wrong . . . but with a bit more money spent on it it really could go up a class, I'm sure. Rodger Farrant and the rest of the management team there are certainly steering it that way and I've no doubt that they'll get there. At the other end of the scale I also have a lot of time for Windsor. Well-run. Scenic. I've had plenty of winners there.

It's a strange fact but more often than not the first time I ever go to any particular course, I win. Don't ask me why. And that's what happened when I took two horses up to Carlisle while I was at South Hatch. Kous and Landski. Both won. Both ridden by Billy Newnes. (Actually, I had been up to Carlisle once before. I was out of luck though, didn't have a runner. Half an hour before the first race the meeting was abandoned!)

But I remember going up to Carlisle for another reason too. After Landski won the Whinlatter Stakes, so landing the double for me (Kous had won the Scania Trucks Selling Stakes earlier on the card) I had a few glasses of champagne in the bar to celebrate. But I couldn't hang around too long; Billy and I had a train to catch. So off I went to fetch Billy. What does he tell me? He's only gone and got himself a spare ride hasn't he. Billy, you're out of your mind. We've got a ******* train leaving in forty minutes! Jesus! I couldn't believe it. He was going to be on the course for another half an hour, at least. Anyway, I told him that I was off; whatever he wanted to do I couldn't wait, I had to catch this train. 'Hold it up for me,' he said. 'Delay it.'

I got to the station at about 3.15. The train was due to leave at 3.42. Just my luck: it's early. It's standing there at the platform. Brilliant! So it's going to be leaving bang on time isn't it.

3.30 comes and goes. Still no sign of Billy. 3.40 and he still isn't there. People are waving goodbye to each other by now, I've got my bags on board and doors are beginning to be banged shut. Still no sign of Billy. But what have I done? I've spotted a shopping trolley on the platform. I don't know what possessed me but I leapt off the train, grabbed this things and – whack! – wedge it in one of the doors. I don't know to this day how I wasn't seen but I wasn't. I suppose the last thing that anyone was expecting was for anyone to do something as stupid as that. Anyway the guard on the platform was slamming more of the doors shut by now. He sees the trolley stuck in this doorway. He and a couple of his mates started trying to wrestle it out. How the **** did this get here? It's now 3.45. And here comes Billy at long last. He jumped on the train just as it started moving off. As we pulled out of the station we looked back at the bent and beaten trolley lying on the platform, these guards still shaking their heads about how it had come to be stuck in a doorway like that.

For Billy though that was the second close call of the

day. He almost threw the race away on Landski when he mistook a path across the course for the finishing line. In fact, the winning post was another seventy-five yards away. Billy stopped riding for a couple of strides, realised his mistake and then got going again. He only just held on. He got Landski home by a short-head from the fast-finishing odds-on favourite Sally Says So. Just as well. It might have been Billy Newnes who ended up bent and beaten on the platform otherwise.

I'll always remember that trip up to Carlisle.

I've often been accused of turning racing into a circus. Because of the clothes that I wear. Because of the way that some of my horses have looked with their day-glo nose-bands and so on. It doesn't bother me though. I'm used to that sort of reaction from the old-school-tie crowd. And every time they say "Look what he's wearing now," I think "Bloody hell. Look at you. Not only do you all look completely the same, you look bloody boring." It just doesn't bother me.

I once wore a multi-coloured ski-suit to Devon and Exeter. Some of these old duffers there went crazy. But I wear what I want to wear and that's it. That particular day it was freezing so I wanted to wear something that was warm, that did the job. I didn't want to wear something just for the sake of it, just to look like everyone else – like they did. But what really amused me was that they were the ones who were shivering out there, complaining about how cold it was. Stupid.

Once I got into trouble at Ascot. *The Sporting Life* had run a caption competition. The photograph that they printed showed a man in top hat and tails reading a paper at the races. Standing behind him there's this punk-rocker: mohican haircut, leather-jacket, the lot. The winner was a man from Guernsey. He earned himself a day at Ascot and a bottle of champagne. His caption: Rod Simpson's gone

147

right over the top this time. Anyway, *The Sporting Life* asked me to present the bottle of champagne to him at the meeting. As it happened I was going to be there anyway, doing some corporate entertainment work in the marquee, so I was only too happy to. I decided that it would be a good laugh to dress up as a punk-rocker, do it like that. I told The Hon. Peter Beaumont, the Clerk of the Course. He wasn't happy. You're not doing that. You're not going to walk through the Royal Enclosure like that, anywhere. You're not doing it. If you do I'll throw you off. Well that settled it. Off I went, got changed in the toilets. I put on chain and studs, a mohican-haircut wig, the works. Out I came to present the winner with his bottle of champagne. He loved it. *The Sporting Life* loved it. And Peter Beaumont didn't hold it against me in the end either. It was a bloody good laugh. The people who I'd been speaking to earlier, while I was all dressed up 'in a whistle' and looking like a trainer is supposed to look, must have thought that I'd gone completely off my coconut.

Favourite horses? Fortune's Guest would definitely have to be one of those. What a character that horse was. He was the rogue of rogues and the prat of prats. He drove me round the bend at times that horse, but I loved him.

You do grow attached to some horses. And another horse which I grew very attached to was Pinctada. He was a lovely horse. But as I've already said, he wasn't very sound. It was a wonder we got him racing at all. It's with horses like that that you really appreciate the work that your staff put in. We won 13 races with him in all. Eleven on the Flat, two over jumps. That was quite an achievement. That we could seriously go for the William Hill Horse of the Year with him, that we came so close to actually winning the title, was little short of a miracle. And during that spell he was running so well too. You would never have know that he had so many problems. During his races he was always going really sweetly. In fact, that worried me quite a bit. Pinctada had this huge white face. He was too easy to pick out. Wherever he was in a race, you could see him. You could see how well he was going. And so could the handicapper, of course. I seriously thought about sooting him up a bit (Pinctada that is, not the handicapper) so that he might be a little less noticeable.

In the end, Pinctada's problems caught up with him. It those brittle bones of his which finally killed him. In his last race at Chester he was pulled up after going lame. And it was obvious even then that it was something pretty serious. Really, we should have had him humanely put down right there and then on the racecourse, but I just had to try and save the old git if I possibly could. It just didn't seem right to let him go like that. "Just try and bear with it a bit longer," I tried to tell him. He was in terrible pain. We took him by horse ambulance to the Leahurst Veterinary Unit at Liverpool. He was given painkillers, had the leg immobilised. It was no good though. The vets decided that the injuries he had sustained – a fractured sesamoid bone and torn check ligaments and main tendon flexor – were just too severe. The following day they put him down. I cried like a baby. For weeks afterwards I couldn't train properly. The staff lost interest too. Grief. That's what it was. We grieved for the horse, bless him.

I still miss Pinctada to this day.

DEJA-VU

When I first moved into Fox Hill Farm, Foxhill, near Wanborough (just outside Lambourn), I thought I'd maybe
give it a year, see how I got on. It was then that I first
thought of writing this book, thinking that perhaps I really
might have to wrap it all up still. As it turned out, things
went quite well. That first year was pretty quiet (I ended
up with 3 winners over the jumps during the '90 – '91
season), but you expect that. A lot of the horses were
struck down with the virus. But, again, that's something
you expect. Moving into an old yard like Fox Hill, that sort
of thing is bound to happen. It's inevitable. There's God
knows what going to come crawling out of the woodwork.
Quiet or not though, things kept ticking over reasonably
enough.

It was on Saturday February 2nd 1991 that I had my first
winner since moving to Foxhill. Rouyan, who had previously been a 3 length fourth to Fidway in the Gerry
Fielden Hurdle at Cheltenham and then a 13½ length
fourth to Crystal Spirit in the Bishops Cleeve Hurdle at the
same course, won the Tote Jackpot Hurdle at Sandown at
8–1, ridden by Billy Morris. He led two out, always having
been up with the pace. He was then headed approaching
the last but ran on again. In the end he won by three-
quarters of a length from Yaheed, Gay Ruffian and King's
Curate. Bradbury Star was fifth. That really did give me a
boost. It proved to people that I could still win a big
handicap. And, again, I'd had a good bet on him. The only
sad note concerning Rouyan was that soon afterwards I
lost him. He was moved to Jenny Pitman.

In my first year at Foxhill I managed to get all of my two year-olds placed. That wasn't bad. It said to all of those people who thought that I might have gone under, owners who were still holding off from sending horses to me: Look, I'm still here. And, look, I can still do the job. Okay, I only had a handful of winners, six, but you can only have the winners if you've got the horses. I made the most of what I had. And I did have winners.

I had some beautiful gallops to work my horses on at Foxhill. Lovely views across the Marlborough Downs. Good, clean air. I had all the facilities to do well. Things actually looked quite rosy. I had some fantastic owners too. People who had stood by me. People like Mr. and Mrs. Painting, for example. Terrific people to have on your side. The yard itself was another considerable plus. Deja-Vu was pleasant, peaceful. It was a cheerful place. And that's how I like things. I like a cheerful attitude to come out in my horses. I think that if you're a miserable son of a bitch then nine times out of ten your horses will be the same.

We were six miles outside Lambourn at Foxhill so we didn't see people quite as often as we had done while we had been at Near Down. Being out of sight we were, perhaps, a little out of mind. But that was okay. We were still as friendly with everyone. In 1990 we'd been along to Kim Bailey's party to celebrate Mr. Frisk having won the National. Two years on we were at Nick Gaselee's celebrating Party Politics having won the race. If I wanted to see anyone, have breakfast with John Francome or whatever, I just had to pick up the phone. No problem.

Charity-work was something I became quite heavily involved in while I was at Near Down. I organised quite a few events to aid the disabled. I raised money for charities and for the injured jockeys Jessica Charles-Jones and Sharon Murgatroyd. It was hard work, but worth it. With the help of Richard Hannon's secretary Judy Horton and professional golfer Ian Bolt, I organised a Golf Day for Jessica. It took nearly five months to set up in all. But we raised £10,000 in the one day. Later, for Sharon's benefit, I got a football team together. It was Johnny Francome (again) who first told me that he and a few of the others had started having a bit of a kick-around on a Sunday morning. Him, Oliver Sherwood, Charlie Brooks . . . some jockeys, stable lads, lads from the pub. People like that. I started going to the rec' to join them. After a while I took John aside and suggested that we set up a proper team, raise some money for charity. I phoned Peter Shilton and asked him if he could send me any kit (footballers are often closely involved with racing and Peter certainly is). Because of my leg, I was going to play in goal. By return of post he sent me a jersey, shorts, gloves, the lot. When I put it all on I even looked like him! A little while later I bumped into the Bournemouth manager Harry Redknapp at the races with some of his players. I asked him for some stuff. He sent me a whole set of white Bournemouth Town shirts. Meanwhile, the ex-jockey Barry Wright, whose brother is attached to Leicester City, gets us a full set of socks and shorts. We were away. Even though there were then only three recognised trainers in the team – me, Oliver Sherwood and Paul Cole who played for us occasionally (plus John Francome, perhaps, who had been a trainer for a while) – we called ourselves the Trainers' Eleven. We won our first game. We beat Allied Dunbar 10–0. By the end of the season we'd played 18, won 14, drawn 1, lost 3. We lost one of those games 1–0. We should have won. That would have made our record even more impressive. Un-- fortunately, Graham McCourt injured himself slightly and had to go off. My son Robin came on as substitute. Then I had to go off after pulling a hamstring. We were unlucky. We were robbed. We would never have lost if I had been able to stay on the pitch. I played left-back most of the season. Oliver Sherwood played in goal in the end. He was a lot better than me, could actually catch the ball. Simon Whitworth was playing for us. John Francome played a leisurely but competent midfield role. Before each game we had a whip-round. Afterwards we would raffle a ball which had been signed by some big club. Manchester United. Leeds United. Whoever. I wish we'd got one from Crystal Palace; I'd have had it. Maybe some other time. The team's still together.

But back to the horses. The '91 – '92 N.H. season proved a highly successful one for me. With only twelve horses in the yard, I notched up 9 winners. Falcon Flight won twice and so too did Xhai, Freezing and Stage Player. The other winner was Manzoor Sayadan.

While I was at Near Down Billy Morris rode a lot of my horses. And, of course, he rode Rouyan when he won the Tote Jackpot at Sandown. But that was while I was giving my usual jockey, Dean Gallagher, a measure of freedom in the hope that he might come in for some more outside rides. Dean Gallagher is a first rate jockey and I didn't want to stand in his way if a better offer came his way. The situation was that I got Billy in as a temporary replacement. Come the '91 – '92 N.H. season Dean was back with me. He was getting rides from Jenny Pitman, Albert Davison and others but basically he was back in the role of being my principal jockey. I explained the situation to Billy. Dean was always going to be my first-choice jockey if he was available. In addition to that, if I didn't continue to 'showcase' his talents, give him the rides that he needed, how was he going to sustain his career? Okay, so Billy had his career to think of, but he also had his paper-bedding business. It wasn't his bread-and-butter in the same way that it was with Dean. What could I do? Anyway, I had to lay him off. I took a lot of stick for it. Billy's wife, Candy, who had ridden a winner on Xhai, found it difficult to stay on with me. She left. It was upsetting, but these things happen. It was one of those situations where whatever decision you come to, someone's going to be disappointed. So . . . Billy left. Dean started riding for me on a regular basis again.

I think Dean Gallagher could be champion jump jockey someday – if he's allowed to be. The thing is, you don't just need the right skills, the right attitude, the right character; you need the rides. That's what it all comes down to in the end. If you don't get those, that's it. Gone. Forget it. But Dean certainly has the skills, the attitude and the character. He has tremendous potential. Like his cousin, Mark, Dean rode on the Flat to begin with. At over 9st though he's heavy. It was inevitable that he would have to change to jumps. But that Flat experience (and he rode a number of winners on the Flat) has given him that extra bit of polish, that extra bit of style. On December 6th 1992 he rode a horse of mine called Freezing at Doncaster. Freezing went off favourite, even though he had fallen in his previous race. Coming to win his race, Freezing hit the final hurdle and Mark Tompkins' Green Glow took the lead on the run-in. It looked to be all over. Dean didn't panic though, didn't flap. But then he didn't accept the situation either. He gathered Freezing up, got her running again, won on the line. Brilliant. Even I thought he had lost it. And I bet most people watching the race thought he had too. Jockeys like Dean are priceless. It might take me three months to present a horse to a race. A poor jockey could cock it all up in three seconds. That's not something that I have to worry about with him.

One of the best things that happened to me while I was at Foxhill was that Palacegate Racing, a racing club which has several horses in training with Jack Berry on the Flat, decided to move into National Hunt as well. They bought Freezing for me at the auctions, claimed Falcon Flight from John Mackie's yard after the horse won at Stratford. Freezing has since been sold, but both horses progressed well (and, as I've already said, won two races each). I hope that my relationship with Palacegate Racing is going to progress too, that they might send me some more horses to train for them.

The 1992 Flat season was a good one for me too. I had 10 winners. One horse whose efforts particularly pleased me – largely because he was owned by Mr. and Mrs. Painting – was the sprinter Olifantsfontein. He won two on the trot, the first at Sandown when he came in at 20–1. That really was good. All the more so, in fact, because I hadn't thought he was quite right that day. He led virtually from the off, went clear, never really looked like being caught.

The Flat season came to an end . . . and so, too, did my two year lease at Foxhill. The rent was put up. With only twelve horses in my care there was no way I could pay it and survive. Once again I was left standing on the brink, facing the very real possibility of having to pack it all in. I had nowhere to go. Offers of jobs (in Dubai and Canada, for example) came to nothing. By mid-October I still didn't know what I was going to do next. My lease ran out on November 1st. Jenny Barons, David Barons' estranged wife, was moving in.

In the fortnight or so that was left to me I finalised arrangements to rent a small yard back in Lambourn from Nicky Henderson: Bourne Stables.

HOLDING ON

Aside from my work as a trainer I'm also involved in quite a few other activities these days. I do a fair bit of corporate entertainment work, for instance, for a company called *Cavendish*. They're really an excellent company, treat their clients and the celebrities who they use (people like me!) really well. Johnny Francome introduced me to them initially shortly after I moved to Near Down. He worked for them. On this particular occasion he had been double booked. I stood in for him. It's one of the best things he's ever done for me. The fact is, without other interests such as this, I doubt whether I would have survived. Even so, I'm still in the situation where I have to play everything by ear, keep taking stock of things. There's no guarantee that I can continue to survive. Times really are hard. You begin to wonder just how much longer you can continue to keep coming back from all the knocks, all the kicks and setbacks that you have to take. When we left Foxhill I felt really fed up, I have to admit. I felt I really couldn't go on living like a nomad, moving from one yard to the next every few years, putting my family through all the hardships such a lifestyle involved. When Eileen and I then realised that our marriage was cracking under the strain and she told me that she was thinking of moving out, I thought maybe it was time that I got a proper job.

But what's that? What is a proper job? The fact is, you have pressures whatever line of work you're in.

Will I ever stop training? I doubt it. What are the alternatives? I can't see me getting a Jockey Club appointment somehow. I'd love to work in television. John Francome and co. have made *Channel Four Racing* really quite exceptional. Perhaps I could help shake things up at the BBC? Somehow I doubt that that's going to happen either. Perhaps I could get further involved in corporate entertainment? I like meeting people. I like people. I like people liking me. There just isn't the opportunity though. And at the end of the day, if I did give up training, I know that I would miss it too much. Eileen has always said that I would curl up and die. I think she's probably right. People have often asked me why I stay in racing when it has given me so many knocks. The reason is simple. I just love the game. I ******* love it.

Regrets? I have a few. Principally though, I think I've been unlucky. Other people's financial problems have directly affected me without me being able to do anything about it. Three times I've been down. Hard knocks. Very hard knocks. Three times I've had to pick myself up again. And that's not to take all of the other blows and niggles into account, all of the other problems that have come my way over the years. Who knows, perhaps I'd be training a string of a hundred or more horses if things had worked out differently. Perhaps I'd be driving around in a Merc or something instead of the clapped-out old banger I have got. Mind you, that's going; I'm getting an XJS or something soon. You can't let things slide. If you possibly can, you have to go for it. Perhaps I could be throwing huge staff parties to show how much I appreciate everyone's efforts. I'd like to. But things haven't worked out like that. So it goes. Basically I'm still a hand-to-mouth trainer. I wasn't a millionaire when I started out and I'm not one now. But I am still in business and unlike a lot of trainers, many of them much wealthier than I am, I'm still on the inside looking out rather than on the outside looking in. I would be lying if I didn't admit that I do feel a little bitter, a little envious of some other trainers on occasion though, trainers who are more successful than I am, who are regularly winning big handicap and group races. I don't like it but the feeling is there. I also realise, as I've already pointed out, that racing has adversely affected my family life. We haven't really had proper holidays together. Eileen goes down to Cornwall with Robin and Rebecca, I'm usually working, can only get down there for the odd day or two. I don't see enough of Robin and Rebecca. I haven't seen enough of Eileen. Racing has certainly taken it's toll on my family relationships, no doubt about it. The fact is though that if you want to train horses there are sacrifices to be made. It is demanding. It is time-consuming. There's no getting away from that fact. Last winter, for instance. I might start work at 6.30 am I muck-out, tack-up. From 7.30 until about 9.00 I'm out on the gallops riding work. The Ascot Sales might be starting at 9.30. But still I need to do my entries, speak to some of my owners, speak to the vet. It can't all be done. I grab a piece of toast, my coat and I'm off (in my clapped-out car). I get to Ascot, buy a horse. It's 11.30. Then I might have to go to some nearby stud to look at a foal that one of my owners is a bit worried about. That afternoon I'm going to Newton Abbot where I've got a runner. I get there sometime after 3.00 after a bloody long drive. I saddle up the horse ready for the 3.45, tell my jockey what to do. If I'm lucky I win. I might be back home by 7.30. I grab my work-book. I work on that, ready for the next day. It's tiring. I go to bed much earlier than in my Funky Flipper days, that's for sure.

Going back to the subject of football which I brought up in the previous chapter. There's always someone in the Trainers' Eleven who gets the ball, gets carried away and wastes it. The rest of us then start shouting Me! Me! Me! Me! It's a bit like that writing your autobiography. You can all too easily get carried away. And that's not the note that I want to end on here. When it comes right down to it I've been lucky really. Very lucky. Unlike most people I've been able to do a job I love. I've found myself in some horrible positions, sure, but I'm still holding on, still here. It's the same for everyone, I think; you just try and make the best out of whatever situation you find yourself in. Jesus, I even play a round of golf some afternoons.

So far, and even though I say it myself (I'm allowed to; it's my book), I think I've done a pretty good job of making the most of whatever situation I've found myself in. Against all of the odds perhaps I haven't been beaten yet. Think positive, that's what I always say.

1993 hasn't started out too badly for me. On Tuesday 12th January my Palacegate Racing horse, Falcon Flight, reappeared in the Guy Mannering Claiming Hurdle at Lingfield, ridden by Dean Gallagher. He went off 2–1 favourite. Always prominent, he took up the running three out and then went clear to win by four lengths from Mister Lawson. My first runner of the New Year a winner. Just over a week later, on January 21st Lyn's Return won the Pennywise Maiden Hurdle (Div. II) – again, at Lingfield – ridden by Steve Smith Eccles. What a start.

But it is only a start. Bourne Stables represents another stop-gap arrangement for me, that's all; I need to find somewhere more permanent if I can. Not only in order to settle the horses, but also because I need to get a little stability into my life if I'm to hold my family together. And that's something which I'm quite determined to do. If things do work out I'd like to move to a new yard, Rusley Park, which is back out towards Foxhill (and where I'd then use the same grass gallops that I used while I was at Near Down). But even if I can get in there I then have to make a success of things, of course. I have to keep the winners coming.

Looking out into the yard now it's impossible not to feel positive about things. I've got some nice animals with me at the moment. Mr. and Mrs. Painting have got four horses with me: The Power of One (who seems to be over the lung problems which affected him last year and is

159

looking quite magnificent), Olifantsfontein, Helios and a new arrival, Sterretjie. I've got a Ken Higson horse (formerly owned by Lord Carnarvon), Warm Spell. There's Palacegate Racing's Falcon Flight, of course. I've got Walk The Beat, who won as a two year-old at Edinburgh last season, Lyn's Return, Grand Applause, Cheshire Annie. All exciting prospects one way and another. If they can do the business then I'll still be in business. It's as simple as that.

How they run will determine just how much of a struggle I'll still have to put up to survive as I am; as a small trainer who loves his family and his horses and just wants to hold them all together.

It's always a struggle. Mainly fun and horses? Not always. But that's my life. I'll make it work. Despite everything, I'm looking forward to the challenges which face me. I've faced many of them before and risen to the occasion. With a little luck, I'll do so again.